Wild, Wild World of Animals

Reptiles
& Amphibians

A TIME-LIFE TELEVISION BOOK

Produced in Association with Vineyard Books, Inc.

Editor: Eleanor Graves
Senior Consultant: Lucille Ogle
Author and Text Editor: Richard Oulahan
    Associate Text Editor: Bonnie Johnson
    Assistant Editors: Regina Grant Hersey, Peter Ainslie
    Literary Research: Ellen Schachter
    Text Research: Nancy J. Jacobsen
    Copy Editor: Robert J. Myer
Picture Editor: Richard O. Pollard
    Picture Research: Judith Greene
    Permissions: Celia Waters
Book Designer and Art Director: Jos. Trautwein
Production Coordinator: Jane L. Quinson

WILD, WILD WORLD OF ANIMALS
TELEVISION PROGRAM
Producers: Jonathan Donald and Lothar Wolff
Time-Life Television Books are published by Time-Life Films, Inc.
Bruce L. Paisner, *President*
J. Nicoll Durrie, *Business Manager*

THE CONSULTANTS

WILLIAM G. CONWAY, General Director of the New York Zoological Society, is an internationally known zoologist with a special interest in wildlife conservation. He is on the boards of a number of scientific and conservation organizations, including the U. S. Appeal of the World Wildlife Fund and the Cornell Laboratory of Ornithology. He is a past president of the American Association of Zoological Parks and Aquariums.

DR. JAMES W. WADDICK, Curator of Education of the New York Zoological Society, is a herpetologist specializing in amphibians. He has written for many scientific journals and has participated in expeditions to Mexico, Central America, and Ecuador. He is a member of the American Society of Ichthyologists and Herpetologists, a Fellow of the American Association of Zoological Parks and Aquariums, and a member of its Public Education Committee.

JOHN BEHLER, Associate Curator of Reptiles of the New York Zoological Society, has published a number of popular and scientific articles and serves as a consultant to the U.S. Fish and Wildlife Service and the U.S. Customs Service. He is a member of all the major herpetological societies.

RICHARD L. LATTIS, Assistant Curator of Education of the New York Zoological Society, is a herpetologist specializing in reptilian behavior. He is a fellow of the American Association of Zoological Parks and Aquariums and a member of many herpetological societies.

THE AUTHOR

RICHARD OULAHAN has always had warm feelings for cold-blooded reptiles and amphibians. As a boy in Washington, D.C., he kept more than 200 turtles in his backyard, and over the years he has counted numerous lizards, snakes, baby alligators, toads and frogs among his friends. A veteran staff writer, correspondent and editor for *Time* and *Life*, he is presently serving as text editor for this series of books.

Wild, Wild World of Animals

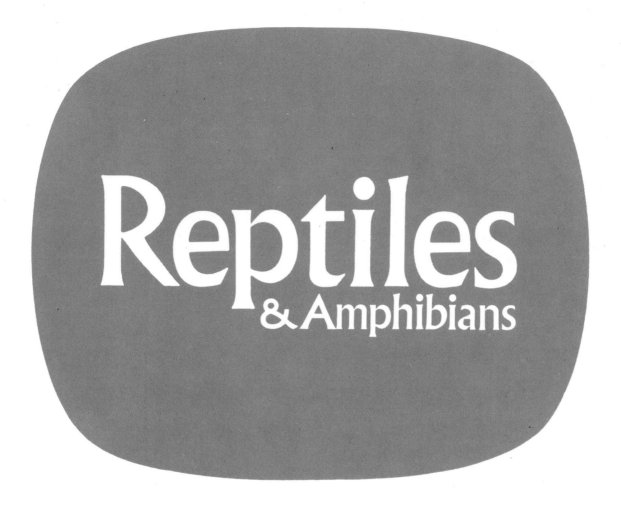

Reptiles
& Amphibians

Based on the television series
Wild, Wild World of Animals

Published by

TIME-LIFE FILMS

© 1976 TIME-LIFE FILMS, INC. All rights reserved.

ISBN 0-913948-06-3

LIBRARY OF CONGRESS CATALOG CARD NUMBER: 76-4658

Contents

Introduction

by Richard Oulahan

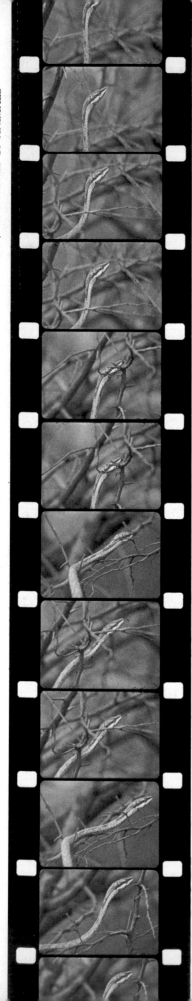

Dᴜʀɪɴɢ ᴀɴ ᴇᴄʟɪᴘꜱᴇ ᴏꜰ ᴛʜᴇ ᴍᴏᴏɴ ɪɴ 1972, Cambodian soldiers stationed in Phnom Penh killed two of their comrades and wounded 83 others when they fired thousands of rounds of ammunition and tracer bullets into the night sky. The fusillade was not an act of war or rebellion; the troops were simply warning the moon that it was being eaten by a snake. According to ancient Khmer legend, the sky is inhabited by an enormous serpent, an evil brother of the sun and moon that attempts to devour its celestial brethren from time to time, and it is the duty of humans during an eclipse to make as much racket as possible in order to alert the sun or moon so that they can escape the dreadful snake's attack. The soldiers in Phnom Penh were simply doing what their parents had taught them to do in early childhood.

That such mythic beliefs persist in an age when men have walked on the moon is not surprising. Humans have been in awe of reptiles and amphibians and have attributed magical powers to them throughout recorded history, simply because they are so different from the other creatures of the earth. They inspire either fear and revulsion or awe and admiration that often escalate to religious worship. However, such reactions are neither inborn nor instinctive. A very young American child will show no fear on his first encounter with a snake, but his older brother will have been taught that a snake is a dangerous, loathsome creature, to be avoided or killed. At the same time, youngsters in certain tribes of Africa and India are taught that the awesome python is sacred, to be respected and worshiped as a god.

It is true that some amphibians and reptiles are potentially dangerous: snakes with fangs that can kill in a matter of minutes or coils that can crush the life out of an animal as large as a deer, crocodiles capable of amputating a leg or swallowing a child, turtles that can snap off a finger or a hand, even poisonous lizards, frogs and salamanders. But, as with so many kinds of animals, the truly dangerous ones are a minority that give the others a bad name. While most reptiles and amphibians are harmless creatures, all are useful to mankind and the earth in keeping the balance of nature.

Still, man has reacted with panic and dread ever since his first encounter with a yawning croc or a writhing snake in some primeval forest millions of years ago. This has given rise to the greatest body of legends and tall tales to surround any group in the animal kingdom. Almost without exception the stories are untrue. There is, for example, no such thing as a hoopsnake that grasps its tail in its mouth and turns itself into a rolling wheel. Glass snakes (which are actually legless lizards) cannot fragment and then miraculously reassemble their bodies. Salamanders are not impervious to fire, and no one ever got warts from handling a toad. Snakes are not slimy, and mother snakes do not protect their babies by holding them in their mouths when danger threatens (although mother crocodiles do carry their young from the nest to the water gently cradled in their mouths). And St. Patrick, remarkable man though he undoubtedly was, did not drive all the snakes out of Ireland. Before snakes could get there from their southern places of origin, the Emerald Isle became detached from the European continent. England became an island in a later period of geologic upheavals, and three kinds of serpentine

8

The crocodile was the inspiration for the dragon in this embroidered Chinese medallion.

invaders were part of the English scene before it separated from the mother continent.

Reptiles—the word is of Greek origin meaning "to crawl"—have been worshiped as gods or supernatural creatures with magical powers like that Cambodian flying snake since the beginning of recorded time. The ancient Egyptians considered the Nile crocodile divine and built a holy city, Crocodilopolis, in its honor. The Aztecs revered Quetzalcoatl, the plumed serpent, as "the master of life." Aphrodite, the Greek goddess of love and beauty, had a sea turtle as an adviser, and across the world Benzai-Teu, the Japanese goddess of learning, eloquence and conjugal bliss, was depicted with a tortoise as her constant companion. The imperial Chinese dragon is believed to be a crocodile.

Ophiolotry, the worship of snakes, is by no means a dead religion. It is still practiced in Punjab and the Malabar Coast in India, and, on the Malaysian island of Penang, the Temple of the Snake is a famous tourist attraction. There, hundreds of snakes, many of them deadly poisonous, lie draped over altars, rafters and shrubbery by day and come down at night to consume the offerings left by the faithful when the stupor-inducing incense wafts away. In equatorial Africa the python is regarded as sacred, and men have been burned alive for accidentally killing one of the giant constrictors. The natives of Madagascar believe that the spirits of dead nobles enter the bodies of boas, and whenever a large snake is found after the burial of a prince, it is hailed with great joy and venerated and indulged for the rest of its days. Rattlesnakes are used in the religious dances of the Hopi Indians of the southwestern United States and in the rites of fundamentalist Christian sects of the rural South—occasionally with fatal effects on the handlers.

Although most humans have not turned to reptile worship, mankind does owe a certain debt to these primitive animals. Without reptiles and amphibians there would be no human race as we know it today. The amphibians were the first creatures to emerge from the sea, the first to breathe through lungs, the first to crawl about on legs. Their immediate descendants, the reptiles, including the dinosaurs, were the

10

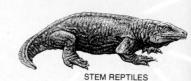

STEM REPTILES

PRIMITIVE AMPHIBIANS

CROSSOPTERYGII

EOSUCHIA

The reptile and amphibian family trees go back to the crossopterygian fishes. The white lines show when the animals existed in ancestral forms; the red lines show when the orders arose in their present forms. Frogs and toads appeared during the Jurassic period. Salamanders evolved later, in the Cretaceous period. The third surviving amphibian order, the caecilians, are of comparatively recent origin. The chelonians, the thecodonts and the eosuchians, as well as all modern reptiles, evolved from the so-called "stem" reptiles. The Chelonia include today's turtles. The Thecodontia were the forebears of the saurischian, pterosaurian and ornithischian dinosaurs and were also the ancestors of modern crocodilians. One branch of the Eosuchia evolved into today's lizards and snakes, while another produced the tuatara, a solitary relict of an ancient world.

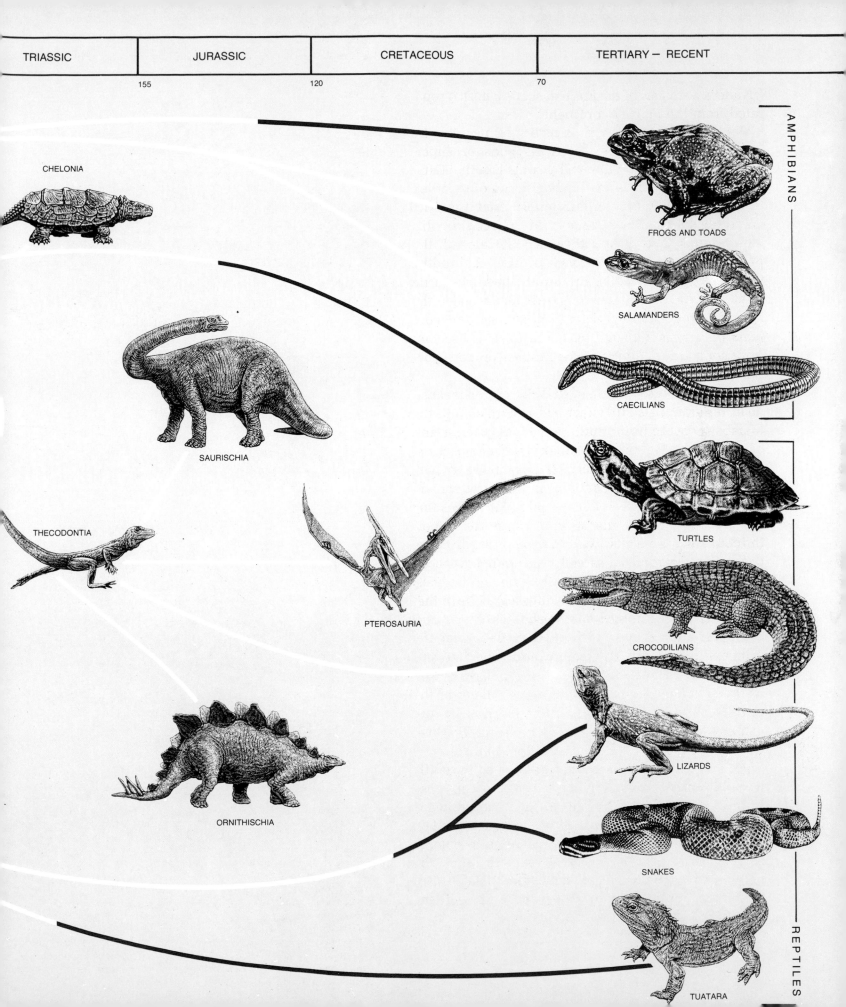

TRIASSIC JURASSIC CRETACEOUS TERTIARY − RECENT

155 120 70

AMPHIBIANS

REPTILES

CHELONIA

FROGS AND TOADS

SAURISCHIA

SALAMANDERS

CAECILIANS

THECODONTIA

TURTLES

PTEROSAURIA

CROCODILIANS

ORNITHISCHIA

LIZARDS

SNAKES

TUATARA

Toad

Frog

Lizard

Snake
Smooth scales

Snake
Keeled scales

As the ancestors of today's reptiles and amphibians spent more time out of water, they had to evolve ways of cutting down their bodies' water loss. One adaptation is reflected in the skins of modern reptiles and amphibians (above). Most toads have skins covered with wartlike protuberances. The skins of frogs are generally smooth, soft and moist. The skins of both frogs and toads contain glands that secrete a mucus that helps prevent them from drying out. Lizards and snakes evolved a horny epidermal covering that slows down evaporation. These plates, or scales, may overlap or abut one another and may be smooth or have a keel down the center.

first vertebrates to live entirely on the land. Every living land animal of today—all the birds of the air, every warm-blooded mammal, including man—is descended from those pioneering amphibians and reptiles.

Until 80 million years ago the reptiles were the dominant animals of the planet, like Quetzalcoatl "the masters of the earth." The Age of Reptiles lasted a full 120 million years, and before that, in the late Devonian period (300 to 350 million years ago), the ancestral amphibians were the only living creatures, other than insects, that evolved separately—sluggish animals that plodded from pool to pool in the steaming swamps, feeding on the huge dragonflies that hovered overhead.

Unlike the so-called warm-blooded mammals that followed them, the reptiles remained "cold-blooded" in that their body temperatures were governed by the temperature of their habitat, which made them unable to tolerate extremes of cold or heat. They developed protective scales that did not require moisture, as the naked skin of amphibians does, and their limbs evolved into a different positioning off the belly, enabling reptiles to move more efficiently on land. The major point of departure from amphibious life, though, was the evolution of a tough-shelled egg, which required no watery hatchery and enabled reptiles to leave their moisture-dependent pasts and become the first completely terrestrial creatures.

Reptiles flourished and dominated the earth for at least 120 million years, adapting to every kind of environment—swamps, deserts, forests, grasslands, rivers, lakes, even the sea and the air. Then, at the end of the Cretaceous period, some 80 million years ago, the Age of Reptiles came to an abrupt—in terms of geologic time reckoning—and mysterious end. The story is told in the striated, chalky rocks of the early part of that period. In those rocks hundreds of different kinds of reptile fossils, including those of dinosaurs, have been found. But, in the rocks of later Cretaceous years, the fossils of all the dinosaurs and four-fifths of the other reptiles, including all of those that flew, completely disappeared.

What caused this dramatic and abrupt extinction? Scientists have theorized and debated the question ever since they learned to interpret the riddles of the Cretaceous rocks, without reaching a completely satisfactory explanation. If a flaming supernova scorched the earth, killing all the dinosaurs and most reptiles by radiation, as some have suggested, then why were there even a few survivors? If their bigness doomed the dinosaurs, why did small members of the family also perish? A sudden cooling or warming of the earth's temperature could indeed have accounted for the so-called "time of dying," but it would just as certainly have exterminated the reptiles and amphibians that live on today to refute that argument. And to attribute the sudden obliteration of so many animals to a natural catastrophe is to invite two unanswerable questions: 1) Why was it selective? and 2) Why was it not recorded in the chalky, telltale Cretaceous rocks?

The true cause of the great extirpation will probably never be known, but it must be counted one of the major events in the story of the earth. The end of the Age of Reptiles left great voids in the terrestrial parts of the earth, to be filled by warm-blooded animals in the beginning of the present Age of Mammals.

What remains of the dinosaurs are fossilized bones and eggs in museums. The rest of the reptiles are not much better off: Of 16 orders known to have roamed the earth, only four have survived. Three of these—the turtles, the crocodilians and the lonely tuatara—are in decline, with just 250 species of turtles, 21 crocodilians and a single order of tuatara surviving. Only the fourth order, which includes both lizards and snakes, has continued to proliferate and adapt to a changing world. Snakes, in fact, are the newest suborder of reptiles, descended from the lizards, with a genesis in the Lower Cretaceous period, when the Age of Reptiles was coming to an end. Together the snakes and lizards consist of over 4,700 species, by far the largest, most modern branch of the reptile class.

Given a reasonable chance, the reptiles might continue to live on indefinitely. But they share the planet with man, and man in a few hundred years has visited on them a second "time of dying." Wholesale slaughter of reptiles for their beautifully patterned skins and shells, and for their flesh and eggs, along with the systematic destruction of their environments, have kept the scaly creatures in a steady decline. Some species, such as the great green turtle of the high seas and the unique tuatara, have been so reduced in numbers that they are now belatedly protected animals, teetering on the brink of extinction and surviving only by the sufferance of man.

The more primitive amphibians have fared no better. Through the attrition of the ages and the encroachments of mankind on their humid habitats they have been reduced to just three orders—the frogs and toads, the salamanders and the snakelike caecilians. The rare sirens, two-legged amphibians, are sometimes classified as a separate fourth order, but most herpetologists place them in the salamander order. As the name *amphibian*—"double life" in Greek—implies, they must live in an environment with access to both water and land, and that limitation alone has kept them from developing as successfully as their reptilian kin. And man's relentless development of the land has cut back the living space of amphibians to an alarming degree. In one particularly dramatic example, the entire world of the Santa Cruz long-toed salamander has now shrunk to an area the size of a racetrack. As if that were not enough, amphibians are preyed on quite as relentlessly as any other animal. In 1971 nine tons of leopard frogs were shipped out of Manitoba for use in United States and Canadian laboratories and schools—some 216,000 frogs, at a rate of 50 to 55 cents a pound. A worthy contribution to science, perhaps, but with that kind of depredation, the springtime choruses of the frogs may soon be just a memory.

If the unhappy day comes when the last reptiles and amphibians have departed this earth, it may be a day of reckoning. These creatures are of inestimable value to mankind and other animals for their role in keeping the delicate balance of nature. They are formidable consumers of insects, rodents and other pests. In South America, planters do not harm snakes in their canefields that control the plagues of rats, and any knowledgeable Midwest farmer knows that an insect-gorged toad is a valuable commodity to him. So, on that silent spring day when the last snakes and frogs and lizards disappear forever and the Age of Insects begins, man himself may not be far behind.

13

Snakes

Because they are so very different from other creatures, snakes have always been depicted as evil incarnate. The characterization is unfair. While it is true that a few snakes are dangerous, most are not. A good case can be made for the snake as one of nature's more useful animals, a marvel of evolutionary engineering and a prodigious destroyer of pests, more often an ally of mankind than a menace. This is especially true in the United States, where just four kinds of snakes—rattlesnakes, copperheads, coral snakes and cottonmouth moccasins—are venomous.

This is not to say that nonpoisonous snakes are always friendly, docile animals. Like any wild creatures, they will defend themselves, and even so-called "harmless" snakes will bite if they are molested. But, treated with respect, most snakes present no threat to humans and will avoid any direct encounters.

Most biologists believe that snakes evolved from lizards, losing their cumbersome legs in the process. But there are a number of physical differences that set snakes apart from lizards as separate suborders of reptiles. Snakes have wriggled into nearly every kind of environment in the temperate and tropical areas of the world, including some, such as the high seas, where even the ubiquitous lizard has not ventured. Some snakes, like the yellow rat snake opposite, climb trees. Others glide through the air or burrow in the ground. There are snakes that spend their entire lives in the ocean and never come ashore, even to give birth. Snakes are found everywhere and in every climate except the poles and a few islands that separated from the great land masses before the late-blooming snakes separated from the lizards 150 million years ago. As a suborder, the snakes are among the most successful of reptiles.

The evolutionary streamlining of the snakes has made them creatures of extraordinary efficiency. Those eyes are unblinking because they have no lids; instead, they are covered with clear scales that fit snugly over the eyeballs like contact lenses and protect them from injury. Eyesight is as important to snakes as it is to other predatory animals, although among burrowing snakes, which have no need at all for vision, the eyes have degenerated and are nearly blind. That constantly flickering, forked tongue is neither a stinger nor a hearing aid, as old wives' tales have it. It functions as a remarkable instrument of tasting and smelling. Whenever the tongue flicks out, it picks up odorous particles from the air or ground and brings them to an opening in the roof of the mouth that leads to a pair of internal cavities on either side of the snake's snout. This unusual olfactory and taste sensor, called Jacobson's organ, analyzes the content of the particles and passes the information on to the brain. By means of its Jacobson's organ, a snake can determine, even without a visual image to confirm it, whether it is in the vicinity of a potential mate or possible prey.

Snakes are not equipped with a conventional sense of hearing, so shouting and loud noises do not perturb them. Their skull bones, however, are acutely sensitive to the slightest vibrations in their vicinity. Some snakes have an additional set of sensors—facial pits with sensitive membranes that enable them to detect the slightest heat radiations from warm-blooded prey.

To aid the process of eating, snakes have some other unusual equipment. Unable to tear their food into chunks, they must swallow everything whole; and in order to manage such a feat when the prospective meal is large, their jaws are uniquely hinged (see page 34), allowing the mouth to open to an unusually wide angle. The snake's throat is elastic and can accommodate prey with a girth much wider than the snake itself. And because their bodies can expand as well, some snakes can, with an effort, consume an animal as big or bigger than themselves.

The surface of the scales on the backs of snakes is either smooth or keeled, with a ridge down the center. The ventral or abdominal scales overlap, providing snakes with friction surfaces that enable them to slide across the ground. Ventral scales are controlled by the muscles pulling against the backbone and other parts of the skeleton to push against the irregularities of the ground surface. Snakes also move their entire bodies in a serpentine motion, pushing their scales against the earth. Desert-dwelling snakes use a "sidewinding" motion to negotiate shifting sands. A sidewinder rattlesnake simply lifts up a loop of its body and lunges that part forward, an effort that propels it into sidewise progress. However they get about, though, snakes are the slithering proof that legless locomotion is an efficient way of exploring and utilizing a habitat. With their generally long and skinny, ground-hugging bodies, snakes can traverse with ease terrain that is virtually inaccessible to many two- or four-footed animals.

Yellow rat snake

Serpentine Locomotion

The fact that snakes no longer have functional legs has actually improved the ability of some to move. Some snakes, such as racers and whip snakes, can easily outdistance man over rough terrain. Snakes move by means of four different methods, often used in combination with each other: serpentine, concertina, sidewinder and rectilinear. In serpentine movement, demonstrated in the multiple-exposure photograph of a moving rat snake (below), the snake "swims" along the ground in a series of "S" curves, using sticks, grass or other protruberances for leverage. Concertina movement is similar to an inchworm's progress along a branch, the body springing forward from a tightly coiled "S." In sidewinding, the body touches the ground only at two points, near the head and tail, and literally "unrolls" itself in a looping motion until the head is extended enough to begin another loop. Constrictors and other large-bodied snakes often move in rectilinear or caterpillar fashion, flat scales on the belly gripping the ground while the rear parts of the body and tail are dragged up behind.

The eastern king snake in the sequence above travels along a slender vine by twisting its head forward and around and drawing its entwined body across the vine like a needle pulling a thread. Snakes are able to exploit their habitats much more thoroughly than most limbed animals. Sometimes snakes will employ a combination of motions, adding a vigorous wriggle to speed up a slithering eellike movement, or sidewinding along with serpentine locomotion to get across unstable terrain.

Snakes that live in deserts or other terra infirma, where shifting sand or soil will not provide a solid surface to grip, have evolved the complex motion of sidewinding. The little—and venomous—sidewinder rattlesnake (below) makes its way along a dune in rapidly wriggling, sidling motions, with only two sections of its body touching the sand at any time. Desert-dwelling snakes in Africa and America have separately evolved identical sidewinding locomotion in their similar bleak habitats.

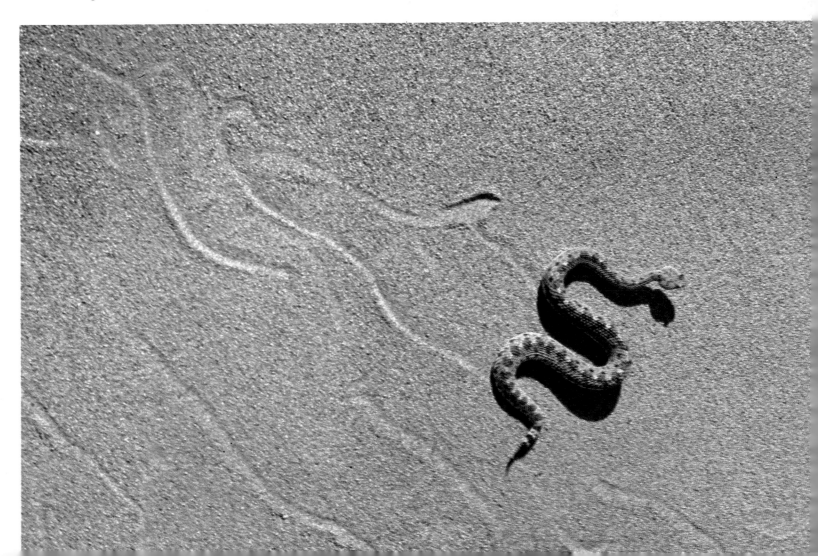

Like many arboreal snakes, the rat snake at left is equipped with flat scales on its underbelly that form ridges and enable it to get a grip on a tree trunk or limb and wiggle steadily in a step fashion up or down in its forest habitat. Despite their great size, anacondas, the largest of the serpents (above), are graceful, sinuous swimmers. Primarily aquatic, they feed on land animals that come to drink from the South American rivers where they live.

The paradise tree snake in the film sequence at right is the famous "flying snake" of Borneo, a member of a small group of serpents that have mastered the first elements of flight. By extending its ribs, the little snake can assume an almost concave, oblong silhouette that permits it to glide through the air as far as 40 yards from one tree to another. The first photographs ever taken of a paradise tree snake in flight are believed to be those recorded in this film sequence.

19

A Hesitant Hatchling

The shells of snake eggs are marvelously constructed of minute, threadlike fibers that form a tough, leathery material, porous enough to allow gases to pass but sufficiently solid to retain the fluids that are vital to the incubation of the baby snakes. At the time it is ready to hatch, each baby is equipped with a tiny "egg tooth" in the front of its snout to enable it to escape into the outside world. The baby corn snake shown here first makes several slits in the shell (left), then squeezes its snout through the opening, finally thrusting its head completely out for a wary look at the world (opposite). It may be several hours before the baby ventures out entirely, and whenever there is any indication of danger it will characteristically withdraw its head into the security of the egg many times before it finally leaves the egg. Some mother snakes remain near the eggs during incubation to guard them from predators, but once the reluctant snakelets are fully hatched, they are completely on their own.

Although the corn snake eggs on these pages are mottled brown in color, they were white when laid and have become covered with dirt. Almost all snake eggs are white or off-white when laid, and since they are always left in a concealed location—customarily in rotten stumps, hollow logs, in the bark debris of fallen trees or in the sand of lakeshores or riverbanks—they have no need for the protective coloring that many bird eggs have. And though no care is provided the hatchlings once they emerge, some female snakes do remain with the eggs until they hatch, leaving during incubation for only brief periods to drink or bathe. Some have even been observed constantly guarding their eggs for as long as 14 weeks. Since snakes are cold-blooded, the females, with a few remarkable exceptions, make no attempt to warm their eggs.

When the corn snake hatchling (left) finally emerges from the egg, its skin will be so moist that particles of dirt will cling to it until, after moving about for a few minutes, it becomes clean and dry. Shortly after hatching—usually between five and ten days—the little snake will shed the skin in which it entered the world. The corn snake, whose warm reds, yellows and browns make it one of the most beautiful of American snakes, grows to be six feet long, thriving primarily on rodents and small birds.

New Skin for Old

The shedding of skin, or ecdysis, occurs almost universally among the higher land animals. The snake is one of the few vertebrates that performs the process in one elegantly complete operation. In birds and mammals, shedding is a gradual, continuous process and may, as in man, be almost imperceptible. But because snakes have a simple, limbless body and lidless eyes, the skin frequently comes off whole, not unlike a stocking being peeled from a leg. The ecdysis process begins from 10 days to three weeks before the actual shedding and is indicated by the snake's loss of appetite (a bloated body might inhibit the process), a bluish cloud over the eyes, a dull cast to the skin and a marked negative turn in the snake's disposition, indicating some discomfort. The eyes clear up a few days before the shedding begins, and then the snake loosens the old skin around its lips by rubbing its mouth against a rough surface. The skin is gradually stripped off the snake as it crawls through rocks and brush, like the ribbon snake below, or as it rubs one part of its body against another. Muscular expansion and contraction and movement of the scales also play an important role. As the skin is worked wrong side out toward the tail, it bunches together and is more easily snagged on passing rough surfaces. The shedding process can take from half an hour to several hours.

The translucent old skin of a European rat snake in the early stages of shedding (right) contains an exact replica of the features on the snake's head, even down to the delicate plates that covered the eyes. The reason the old skin—or shed—is colorless is that, in the process of shedding, only the dead outer layer of the true skin peels off. The pigment cells, which give the snake its color, are deep within the growing part of the skin and give a vivid hue to the newly exposed skin of the rat snake (above), which has completed half of its shedding chores. Frequency of shedding depends on a number of factors, such as age (young snakes shed more often than older ones), temperature (the warmer a snake's environment the more often it sheds, with a 10-degree F. increase in temperature enough to double the rate) and humidity. Although knowledge of shedding frequency is limited, especially for snakes living in the wild, a group of 32 captive rattlesnakes sloughed their skins about four times a year. A reticulated python under observation for 18 years shed on the average of once every 55 days, or almost seven times a year, prompting one naturalist to calculate that if all the sheds were laid end to end they would stretch for a third of a mile.

England Have My Bones by T. H. White

T. H. White, author of over a dozen books on a wide variety of subjects, brings his own brand of eccentricity and gentle irony to the subject of grass snakes in England Have My Bones. *Not many people would consider taking a snake to church, but White does so with aplomb, if without religious benefit to either himself or the snake. Perhaps as a result of his own sharp sense of individualism, White has a deep respect for his reptilian friends, appreciating them simply because they are "inevitably themselves."*

The snakes are about again. Last year I used to go out with Hughesdon to catch them, and then turn them loose in the sitting-room. At one time I had about a dozen. There are four in the room just now.

Grass snakes are fascinating pets. It is impossible to impose upon them, or to steal their affections, or to degrade either party in any way. They are always inevitably themselves, and with a separate silurian beauty. The plates of the jaw are fixed in an antediluvian irony. They move with silence, unless in crackling grass or with a scaly rustle over a wooden floor, pouring themselves over obstacles and round them. They are inquisitive. They live loose in the room, except that I lock them up at nights so that the maids can clean in the mornings without being frightened. The big open fireplace is full of moss and ferns, and there is an aquarium full of water in which they can soak themselves if they wish. But mostly they prefer to lie under the hot pipes of the radiator, or to burrow inside the sofa. We had to perform a Caesarian operation on the sofa last year, to get out a big male.

It is nice to come into the room and look quickly round it, to see what they are doing. Perhaps there is one behind Aldous Huxley on the book-shelves, and it is always worth moving the left-hand settle away from the wall. One of them has a passion for this place and generally falls out. Another meditates all day in the aquarium, and the fourth lives in the moss.

Or it is nice to be working in the arm-chair, and to look up suddenly at an imagined sound. A female is pouring from behind the sofa. As the floor is of polished wood she gets a poor grip on it (she prefers the sheepskin hearth-rug) and elects to decant herself along the angle between wall and floor. Here she can press sideways as well as downwards, and gets a better grip.

She saw our movement as we looked up, and now stops dead, her head raised in curiosity. Her perfect forked tongue flickers blackly out of its specially armoured hole (like the hole for the starting handle in a motor, but constructed so as to close itself when not in use) and waves itself like lightning in our direction. It is what she feels with in front of her, her testing antennae, and this is her mark of interrogation. An empathic movement: she can't reach us, but she is thinking Who or What? And so the tongue comes out. We sit quite still.

The tongue comes out two or three times (its touch on the hand is as delicate as the touch of a butterfly) and flickers in the air. It is a beautiful movement, with more down in it than up. It can be faintly reproduced by waggling the bent forefinger quickly in a vertical plane. Then she goes on with her pour, satisfied, towards her objective in the moss. We sit as still as a mouse.

I try to handle these creatures as little as possible. I do not want to steal them from themselves by making them pets. The exchange of hearts would degrade both of us. It is only that they are nice. Nice to see the strange wild things loose, living their ancient unpredictable lives with such grace. They are more ancient than the mammoth, and infinitely more beautiful. They are dry, cool and strong. The fitting and variation of the plates, the lovely colouring, the movement, their few thoughts: one could meditate upon them like a jeweller for months.

It is exciting to catch them. You go to a good wood, and look for snaky places in it. It is difficult to define these. There has to be undergrowth, but not overgrowth: a sunny patch, a glade or tiny clearing in the trees: perhaps long grass and a bit of moss, but not too wet. You go into it and there is a rustle. You can see nothing, but dive straight at

the sound. You see just a few inches of the back, deceptively fluid for catching hold of, as it flashes from side to side. You must pounce on it at once, for there is no time to think, holding it down or grabbing it by head or tail or anywhere. There is no time to select. This is always exciting to me, because I frighten myself by thinking that it might be an adder. As a matter of fact, there are very few adders in the Shire, and in any case they move differently. An adder would strike back at you, I suppose, but a grass snake does not. It pretends to strike, with mouth wide open and the most formidable-looking fangs; but it stops its head within a millimetre of the threatened spot, a piece of bluff merely.

When you have grabbed your snake, you pick it up. Instantly it curls round your hand and arm, hissing and lunging at you with the almost obtuse angle of its jaw;

exuding a white fluid from its vent, which has a metallic stink like acetylene. Take no notice of it at all. Like an efficient governess with a refractory child, you speak sharply to the smelly creature and hold it firmly. You take hold of its tail, unwind it, roll it in a ball (it is wriggling so much that it generally helps in this), tie it up in your handkerchief, put it in your trouser pocket and look for another.

When you loose it in your sitting-room it rushes off along the floor, swishing frantically but making little progress on the polished wood, and conceals itself in the darkest corner. At night, when you come to lock it up, it makes a fuss. It produces the smell again, and the hiss. In the morning it is the same. Next night perhaps the smell is omitted, or fainter. In a few days there is only a dim hiss, a kind of grumble. This goes as well, until there is only a gentle protesting undulation as it is lifted off the ground.

I remember particularly two of last year's snakes. One was a baby male (the yellow markings are brighter in the male) only about eight inches long. He was a confiding snake, and I once took him to church in my pocket, to make him a Christian and to comfort me during the sermon. I hope it was not an undue interference with his life: I never carried him about like that again, he seemed to like the warmth of my pocket, and I believe he did not change his creed.

Talking of Christians, I never christened the snakes. To have called them names would have been ridiculous, as it is with cars. A snake cannot have a name. If it had to be addressed I suppose it would be addressed by its generic title: Snake.

The other one, I regret to say, was nearly a pet. She was a well-grown female with a scar on her neck. I suppose this had been done to her by man. It was the scar that first attracted me to her, or rather made me take special notice of her, because she was easy to distinguish. I soon found that when the time came for putting her to bed she did not undulate. She never troubled to conceal herself at bedtime, nor to slide away from me when I approached. She would crawl right up to me, and pour over my feet while I was working. There was no horrible affection or prostration; only she was not afraid of me. She went over my feet because they were in a direct line with the place she was making for. She trusted, or at least was indifferent.

It was a temptation. One coldish afternoon she was sitting in my chair when I wanted to read. I picked her up and put her in my lap. She was not particularly comfortable, and began to go away. I held her gently by the tail. She decided that it was not worth a scene, and stayed. I put my free hand over her, and she curled up beneath it, the head sticking out between two fingers and the tongue flickering every now and then, when a thought of curiosity entered her slow, free mind.

After that I used sometimes to sit with my two hands cupped, and she would curl between them on cold days. My hands were warm, that was all.

It was not quite all. I am afraid a hideous tinge of possession is creeping into this account. When other people came into the room she used to hiss. I would be dozing with her tight, dry coils between my palms, and there would be a hiss. The door would have opened and somebody would have come in. Or again, if I showed her to people she would hiss at them. If they tried to catch her, she would pour away. But when I gave her to them she was quiet.

I think I succeeded in keeping my distance. At any rate she had a love affair with one of the males. I remember finding them coiled together on the corner table: a double rope-coil of snake which looked like a single one, except that it had two heads. I did not realise that this was an affair of the heart, at the time.

Later on she began to look ill. She was lumpy and flaccid. I became worried about the commissariat. Snakes rarely eat—seldom more than once a fortnight—but when they do eat they are particular. The staple food is a live frog, swallowed alive and whole. Anybody who has ever kept snakes will know how difficult it is to find a frog. The whole of the Shire seems to be populated by toads: one can scarcely move without treading on a toad: but toads disagree with snakes. They exude something from the skin.

I had been short of frogs lately, and (as I merely kept them loose in the aquarium so that the snakes could help themselves when they wanted) did not know when she had last had a meal. I thought I was starving her and became agitated. I spent hours looking for frogs, and found one eventually, but she wouldn't touch it. I tried a gold-fish; but that was no good either. She got worse. I was afraid she was poisoned, or melancholic from her unnatural surroundings.

Then came the proud day. I got back at half-past twelve, and looked for her on the hearth-rug, but she was not there. She was in the aquarium, sunlit from the french windows. Not only she. I went closer and looked. There were twenty-eight eggs.

Poor old lady, she was in a dreadful state. Quite apathetic and powerless, she could scarcely lift her head. Her body had fallen in on itself, leaving two ridges, as if she were quite a slim snake dressed in clothes too big for her. When I picked her up she hung limp, as if she were actually dead; but her tongue flickered. I didn't know what to do.

I got a gold-fish bowl and half-filled it with fresh grass clippings. I put her in it, with the frog, and tied paper over the top as if it were a jam jar. I made holes in the paper and took it out on to the lawn, in the full glare of the summer sun. Snakes are woken up by heat, and the bowl would concentrate the sun's beams. It was all I could think of or do, before I went in to lunch.

I came back in half an hour. The bowl was warm with moisture, the grass clippings were browning, the frog was gone; and inside was Matilda (she positively deserved a name) as fit as a flea and twice as frisky.

The scarred snake may have been a good mistress, but she was a bad mother. If she had known anything about maternity, she would not have laid her eggs in the aquarium. It seems that water is one of the things that is fatal to the eggs of grass snakes. I picked them out, and put them in another gold-fish bowl, this time full of grass clippings that were already rotten. Then I left them in the sun. They only went mouldy.

She was completely tame, and the inevitable happened. The time came for me to go away for two months, so I gave her her liberty. I took her out into the fountain court (next time it shall be into the deepest and most unpopulated forest) and put her on the ground in the strong July sunlight. She was delighted by it, and pleased to go. I watched her to-froing away, till she slipped into the angle of a flowerbed, and then went resolutely indoors. There were plenty of other things in the future besides grass snakes.

That night I went down to the lake to bathe, and stepped over a dead snake in the moonlight. I guessed before I looked for the scar. I had kept my distance successfully, so that there were no regrets at parting, but I had destroyed a natural balance. She had lost her bitter fear of man: a thing which it is not wise to lose.

I feel some difficulty in putting this properly. Some bloody-minded human being had come across her on a path and gone for her with a stick. She was harmless, useless dead, very beautiful, easy prey. He slaughtered her with a stick, and grass snakes are not easy to kill. It is easy to maim them, to bash them on the head until the bones are pulp. The lower jaw no longer articulates with the upper one, but lies sideways under the crushed skull, shewing the beautiful colours of its unprotected inner side. The whole reserved face suddenly looks pitiful, because it has been spoilt and ravaged. The black tongue makes a feeble flicker still.

These things had been done, to a creature which was offering confidence, with wanton savagery. Why? Why the waste of beauty and the degradation to the murderer himself? He was not creating a beauty by destroying this one. He cannot even have considered himself clever.

King of the Snakes

Though difficult to imagine, looking at this horrifying sequence of pictures, the striped snake on the right (below), the nonpoisonous California king snake, is considered one of man's best friends in the snake world. While stories of the king snake's good deeds, such as saving children threatened by poisonous snakes, are most certainly exaggerations, they do contain a grain of truth. The king snake can coexist with man in rural areas, showing little aggression when encountered and usually making no attempt to bite even when handled. On the contrary, it will coil around a captor's hand and settle down in apparent contentment. When confronted with another snake, however, such as the hapless Pacific rattler seen here, the king snake reveals another aspect of its character—the one from which its name derives. In such a confrontation it is a deadly, almost always victorious combatant that preys on other snakes, even other king snakes. Two common misconceptions about the king snake are that it actively hunts other snakes and that it particularly prefers the venomous varieties. While it is true that snakes make up a portion of the king snake's diet, these meals seem more a result of chance encounters than of specific predatory instincts, for king snakes have a wide range of acceptable food items and will eat rodents, lizards and frogs.

Recent studies show that the king snake is not immune to snake venom but has an apparent tolerance for it. Its aggressive tactics reduce the possibility that it will be bitten, as the Pacific rattlesnake on these pages apparently knows. Rattlesnakes, in fact, have adopted a completely uncharacteristic defensive posture (left), which they use only when confronting a king snake. Rather than coil for a strike at its tormentor, the rattler moves its head as far as possible from the king snake's jaws and throws its midsection or tail at the aggressor. This maneuver is an attempt to thwart the king snake's modus operandi, which invariably begins by gripping the rattler with its jaws a few inches behind the rattler's head. Then the king snake loops its body around the victim and applies pressure until its prey is suffocated. When the struggling ceases, the king snake ingests its victim (above and right) head first, seemingly ''walking'' its gaping, double-hinged jaws around its food.

On the Defensive

Snakes almost always prefer to avoid direct confrontation when they are disturbed or threatened, and as a result they have developed a curious variety of defensive maneuvers, ranging from the outright menacing to the merely comical. Issuing warning noises, such as hissing or rattling, is a common and effective method of discouraging intruders, though there are unusual variations in how some snakes produce these sounds. The saw-scaled viper of Africa and Asia, for example, rubs the saw-toothed scales on the folds of its body against one another to produce a hissing sound. And there are many other snakes that vibrate their tails against dry grass and twigs when disturbed to produce a rattling noise that is audible up to six feet away. The three snakes pictured here—the eastern hog-nosed snake (left and below), the royal, or ball, python (opposite, above) and the ring-necked snake (opposite, below)—have each developed a unique, and amusing, method of dealing with unwanted interference.

The nonpoisonous hog-nosed snake is shown (above and right) in the two stages of its bizarre defensive reactions. In the initial stage (above) it dilates the skin on the rear of its head and neck, creating the hooded effect of an angry cobra. At the same time, the hog-nose inhales deeply, then exhales with an angry hiss and repeated mock attacks. (Such antics have given rise to the hog-nosed snake's common names—puff adder or spreading adder.) If this outburst fails to dissuade the interloper, the hog-nose adopts another tactic (right). It opens its mouth wide, makes its body go limp and rolls over on its back, where it shudders violently until finally it lies motionless. Once the threat has passed, the hog-nose flips over and glides away. In spite of its belligerent behavior, the hog-nose is among the gentlest of snakes, refusing to bite even if a finger is forced into its mouth.

In nature, the royal, or ball, python (left) has the peculiar habit of coiling into a tight ball when frightened or molested—a ball so tightly coiled that it can actually be picked up and rolled.

The southern ring-necked snake (below) is a timid creature rarely reaching 18 inches in length. If disturbed or frightened, the southern ring-neck raises its tail with a twisting motion, revealing a bright reddish or yellowish underside. Such defensive behavior is responsible for its sobriquet in some areas as the corkscrew snake.

A Movable Feast

The swallowing ability of snakes is one of their more amazing adaptations. This capacity for consuming food that is often larger than they are—made possible by the snake's unique, double-hinged jaw—is partially responsible for the dietary rubric in the snake world of a few widely spaced but sizable meals. In captivity, some snakes have refused food for a year or longer, although usually captive snakes will eat small- to moderate-size meals at much more frequent intervals. The problem with oversize meals is that the snake is often handicapped afterward, sometimes to the point of being helpless for several days. This is especially true of larger snakes, which, probably because they are unable to retreat to adequate seclusion for digestion, are more frequently found in this condition. It is a fallacy that snakes lather their food with saliva before ingestion to make swallowing easier. Salivation does occur but only after food has entered the snake's mouth.

Poisonous snakes and constrictors make eating easier by immobilizing their victims before ingesting them, but other snakes, like the common garter snake about to dine on frog's legs and frog (left), consume their prey live, which often results in a struggle to get meals down. The long-nosed tree snake, shown above in a controlled situation, prepares to consume a lizard.

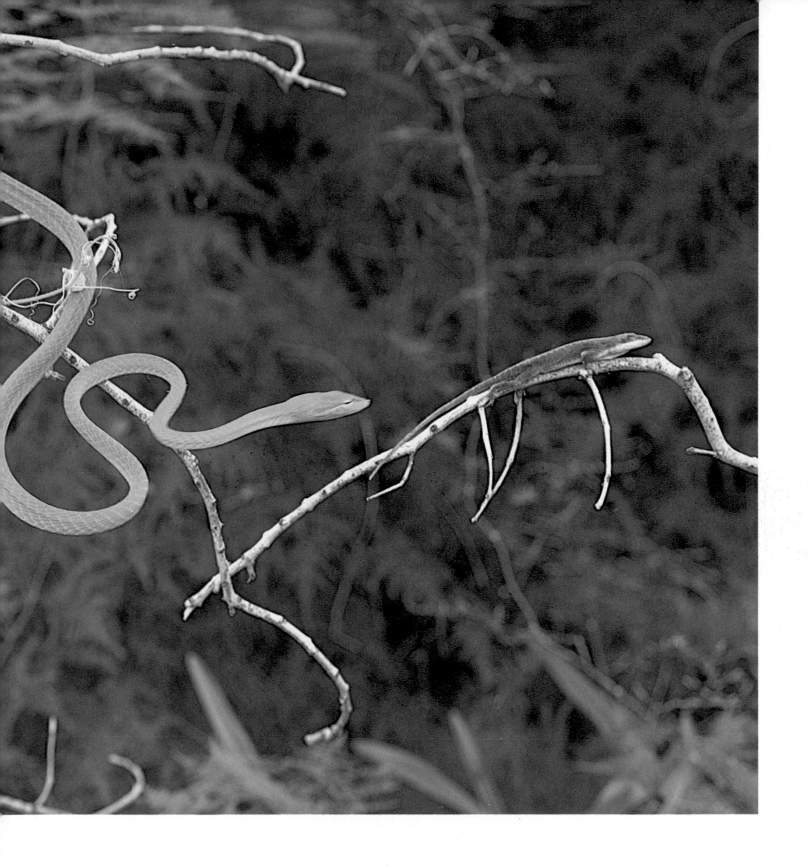

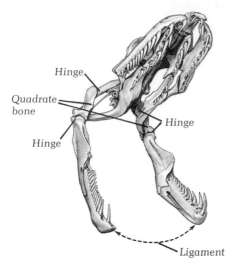

Hinge

Quadrate bone

Hinge

Hinge

Ligament

Reports of a 26-foot anaconda devouring a five-foot caiman or a 14-inch cottonmouth moccasin ingesting a 29-inch ribbon snake could be dismissed as folklore were it not for the remarkable double-hinged jaw that snakes are equipped with. At left is a drawing of the jaw of a reticulated python. This versatile structure enables snakes to drop the lower half of the jaw at a greater angle than a single hinge would allow, giving them the capacity to swallow creatures considerably larger in diameter than themselves. The quadrate bones, which loosely connect the skull to each side of the lower jaw, are hinged at both ends and greatly amplify the snake's oral cavity. The two halves of the lower jaw are not fused in front, as in other vertebrates, but rather are connected by an elastic ligament, which gives them some degree of independence of movement. Therefore, once a victim is in the grip of the snake's backward-curving, or "recurved," teeth, like the toad being consumed by the brown ground snake (below), the snake forces the food toward its esophagus by moving first one side of its mobile jaws and then the other, working rather like the two arms of a man hauling in rope.

Undaunted by an egg more than twice the width of its own body, an African egg-eating snake (left) prepares for a most implausible meal—shell and all. Its few teeth are modest and blunt, of little use beyond gripping an egg (below, left). Once the egg is engorged, forcing the scales on the bloated neck skin to stand far apart (below, right), it comes in contact with another adaptation— the "egg saw," which is a row of six or eight sharp, downward-pointing spines in the rear of the throat. Swallowing motions push the egg against these until it is punctured, whereupon pressure from the distended neck skin collapses the egg at once, sending its contents into the stomach. A valve at the entrance to the stomach rejects bits of shell while retaining the yolk and white inside. Special throat muscles pushing against the ventral column bundle the shell and membrane together, sharp edges inward to prevent scratches, and move them forward for regurgitation.

Splendor in the Grass

The coiled beauties on these pages look as though they had slithered through a paintbox, but for all their vivid colors and intricate markings, the snakes melt marvelously into the surroundings of their natural habitats, where their gaudy coats serve as perfect camouflages. They are, left to right, top row: the rare Arizona king snake, which closely resembles and is often mistaken for the poisonous coral snake; the small green snake, a gentle, insectivorous meadow-dweller; and the milk snake, which gets its name from its presumed but completely mythical ability to suck milk from the udders of cows.

Center row: the rainbow snake; the convict-suited western shovel-nosed snake (the victim of some accident, this specimen has lost one of the forks of its tongue); and the green rat snake, a member of a large tribe named for its ravenous appetite for rats and other rodents.

Bottom row: the San Francisco garter snake, a nearly extinct member of a large and familiar genus; the gray-banded king snake; and the vivid scarlet snake.

The Cosmopolitan Colubrids

The nonvenomous snakes on these pages are members of the principal snake family, the Colubridae, an enormous group that includes approximately two-thirds of the world's snakes, most of which are nonvenomous. Colubrids lack the hind-limb vestiges of the boas and pythons and poison-injecting fangs of the viperids and rattlesnakes, although a few species have grooved teeth in the rear of their jaws for poison delivery. There are 38 genera of colubrids in the United States alone. The angry-looking bull snake, or gopher snake (left), preys on mice, rats, pocket gophers and ground squirrels and is therefore considered a valuable friend of farmers. The black pine snake (below) lives in a restricted region from southern Alabama to eastern Louisiana. Both the bull and the black pine snakes are noisy creatures that hold their ground when disturbed, hissing loudly and making mock strikes rather than retreating quietly.

Rat snakes, like the yellow rat snake (above), are powerful constrictors. The identifying characteristics of these partly arboreal, partly terrestrial snakes include a squarish head and flat belly—so flat as to be almost at right angles with the snake's sides. This structural modification is important, for the rat snake —wedging itself between the ridges of bark on a tree—uses the sharp corners to gain traction and crawl up the trunk. Garter snakes, like the wandering garter snake (left), are among the most familiar of North American reptiles, ranging farther north (to Alaska) than any other snake in the Western Hemisphere. The wandering garter is an insectivore in its youth, but as an adult it feeds primarily on creatures such as earthworms, frogs, toads and salamanders.

The distinctive upturned snout and elongated head at right belong to the long-nosed tree snake of Malaya and the East Indies. The only time these bright green forest-dwellers ever come down to the ground is to lay their eggs. The iridescent pink underside of the snake seen coiled around itself below is that of the Liophidium rhodogaster. This slender snake, which has no common name, is a harmless inhabitant of Madagascar·

The larger nonpoisonous snakes tend to live on or near the ground rather than to be arboreal. One exception is the red-tailed rat snake from Southeast Asia seen opposite and on the cover. It is a slim and agile climber that generally grows to a length of eight feet.

Constrictors

Natives of Guyana tell a tale of a group of hunters who came upon an enormous wall in the middle of the jungle. It was too high for them to scale, so they walked along its side for four days and three nights. And when at last they came to the end, they discovered the head of a gigantic, sleeping snake. Their "wall" was an enormous anaconda 100 or more miles long!

Such monsters exist only in folklore, or perhaps in Loch Ness, but the giant snakes that do exist are impressive enough to stir the imagination of any folklorist. The constrictors kill prey by squeezing it. They come in many sizes, and while most of them grow no bigger than ordinary snakes, the larger members of the family are the biggest snakes on earth.

The family includes both the boas of the New World and the Old World pythons—such as the green tree python shown on the opposite page. The longest of all are the awesome anacondas of South America, which are believed to have reached lengths of more than 37 feet, followed closely by the reticulated pythons, which have been measured accurately at 33 feet. Most of the other members of the constrictor family are relative runts, growing to a length of no more than 18 feet.

The physical differences between the boas and pythons are superficial, and they look very much alike. Most boas are live-bearing, and all pythons lay eggs. As very old forms, dating back to the time when snakes first separated from their lizard ancestors, constrictors retain vestigial legs that appear on the adult as two small spurs. No longer of any use in locomotion, the spurs are believed to serve as positioning and steadying aids for male snakes during sexual intercourse.

In breeding, pythons copulate for as long as three hours. After her eggs are laid, the female python coils her body around them for about three months, until they hatch. Brooding python mothers have the ability to raise their own body temperature as much as 13 degrees F. to warm their eggs—an uncommon phenomenon among cold-blooded animals, whose body temperature is normally governed entirely by their behavior and the external temperature. This built-in thermal control is accomplished by spasmodic muscular contractions, like shivering, that warm up the eggs to incubation temperature.

Strict carnivores, boas and pythons are not at all fussy about their diets and will eat almost any warm-blooded prey, which they find by means of special heat-sensing pits that border their mouths. There have been unconfirmed reports of a python eating an adult leopard and of a 37.5-foot anaconda with the body of a horse in its stomach. Authenticated records disclose some prodigious meals: a 130-pound impala devoured by a 16-foot African python, a full-grown ocelot eaten by a South American boa. The mongoose, that somewhat overrated nemesis of the cobra, is a frequent victim of constrictors. Even porcupines are not safe from a hungry python. By the same token, hungry pythons are not always safe from porcupines. The body of an Indian python was once found with the quills of its porcupine meal sticking through its ribs. In Southeast Asia and Australia, pythons have such an appetite for rats that they are recognized as rodent controls and knowledgeable farmers often lock them in their granaries and storehouses to protect the harvests from the hordes of rats that would otherwise destroy them.

Constrictors ambush their prey, striking swiftly and accurately and quickly wrapping a coil or two around the body, then squeezing ever more tightly until the victim dies of suffocation or compression of the heart. Stories of constrictors crushing their prey to a broken, bloody pulp are myths; bones are rarely broken. Death comes quickly, and the constrictor thereupon seeks out the head, opens and stretches those remarkable jaws and proceeds to ingest its food in a fashion that has been described as "walking over" its food and likened to pulling on an elastic stocking. Constrictors, like all other predators, are quite capable of attacking several victims in rapid succession: One African python was observed with three jackals in its coils.

Constrictors have adapted to many tropical and subtropical habitats. The African python lives in rain forests and semideserts. The South American anaconda spends a great deal of time in the water, while the closely related boa constrictors live mostly in shrubs and on the ground. The reticulated python of India, the Sunda Islands and the Philippines is a skilled swimmer that goes to sea unhesitatingly and is known as an island-settler. After the earth-shaking volcanic explosion that shattered and destroyed most of the Indonesian island of Krakatoa in 1883, the first creature to make its way back to the blasted island was a reticulated python.

New Guinea green tree python

Coiling Aerialists

The weightier constrictors, such as the reticulated python and the anaconda, are restricted in their habitats to the ground and water, but their middleweight cousins, the boas, take to the trees when they are young snakes, and some live out their lives in the treetops. The beautifully marked emerald boa of Brazil and northern South America (below) is almost completely arboreal. Its strikingly vivid coloration is perfect camouflage in the brilliant greenery of the jungle canopy, enabling the boa to slither unobserved through the leaves and vines and strike with lightninglike accuracy at birds, monkeys and other prey, which then become the victims of its powerful coils. A boa characteristically attacks by lashing out at a warm-blooded animal and getting a firm grip on it with its strong teeth, then looping its coils around it and constricting until the victim suffocates.

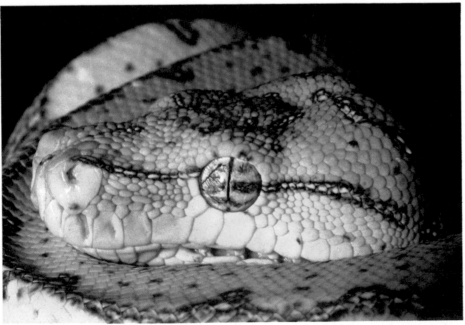

The baleful, unblinking stare of a snake is not, as legend has it, capable of "hypnotizing" potential prey. The green tree python, a native of New Guinea, Australia and the Aru Islands (above), is an aerialist and a nocturnal hunter. In daylight its pupils narrow to vertical slits (left), and after sundown they widen into catlike ovals, enabling the snake to seek out nearby prey. In stalking, pythons are also aided by their Jacobson's organ sensors (see page 14) and by small, rectangular pits on their upper and lower lips, which can detect the faintest heat radiations from warm-blooded animals.

Deadly Embrace

Voluptuously coiled on a log, the rainbow boa (above) is an agile climber of trees and rocky ledges but clumsy on open ground. Its multicolored, intricately patterned skin sheathes a body that is a mass of powerful muscles. Although horror stories about these snakes abound, natives of their Central and South American habitats know that boas are harmless to man, and, in fact, they sometimes keep them as pets. The boa's African cousin, the rock python (opposite), is another matter; it is one of four large constrictors that are capable of killing humans. The other three are the reticulated python and the Indian python of the Old World and the giant anaconda of South America.

When attacking, a constrictor first lashes out and bites its prey with teeth that are firmly set at a backward angle in its mouth; so that a struggling victim cannot disengage itself without tearing its flesh. Next the snake loops a coil or two around the doomed animal and suffocates it in a lethal embrace, as shown in the film sequence at right of a reticulated python constricting a bandicoot rat. With larger constrictors, prey can be sizable. An African rock python, like the one below, once consumed a waterbuck weighing 68 pounds.

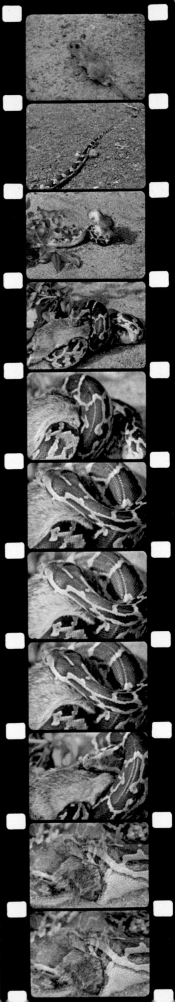

47

Poisoners

Every year around 50,000 people die of snakebite poisoning, 75 percent of them in India, where venomous snakes abound and the human population is among the densest on earth. Some scientists question the dramatically higher death rate in India and wonder whether "snakebite" might be just a convenient term to cover other kinds of death. But even without the questionable Indian statistics the figures still mark the venomous snake as a formidable killer of man. And, as if that weren't enough, there are two kinds of venomous lizards and several dozen tiny frogs and toads that have venom capable of killing humans.

Poisonous snakes are found throughout the world, in deserts and jungles, in mountains up to altitudes of 11,000 feet, in the oceans, as far north as Finland and the Arctic Circle and as far south as Patagonia. In some places, such as the United States, Canada and Europe, venomous snakebites are relatively minor, accounting for considerably less than one-hundreth of 1 percent of the annual death rates. The most venomous species tend to concentrate in the tropical areas of the earth. Australia has the dubious distinction of harboring the largest percentage of venomous snakes anywhere. Sixty percent of the snakes Down Under are potential killers, and they include two of the deadliest species known, the tiger snake and the taipan snake. Even so, the death rate from snakebite is remarkably low.

Which snake is the most lethal? The question is relative, for a snake with venom of relatively low toxicity can kill just as certainly as one with a high potency. Although the degree of toxicity can vary even among individual snakes, the most potent land snake is probably the tiger snake of southern Australia. There are other variables: Some snakes are aggressive and will attack humans or animals; others must be cornered or goaded before they will strike. The fast-moving mambas of Africa have been known to bite any moving thing in their line of sight. But some of the most notorious killers are actually not as dangerous as their reputations suggest. Most cobras will attack only as a last resort, oftentimes striking with their mouths closed. Every "snake charmer" knows that cobras can strike only as far as they are able to lift their bodies off the ground, and the "charmers" always sit prudently out of range of the swaying serpents.

Snakes kill with two kinds of venom—hemotoxins, which kill red blood cells and destroy blood vessels, and neurotoxins, which attack and paralyze the nervous system; both kinds can be equally deadly. To deliver their lethal venom, poisonous snakes are equipped with three kinds of dentition: the short, hollow teeth of the elapids, such as cobras, mambas and coral snakes; the grooved venom fangs located at the back of the mouth, typical of a few members of the colubrid family like the deadly boomslang; and the long, tubular, frontal fangs of the viperids such as rattlesnakes, fer-de-lances and Russell's vipers—the lethal "Speckled Band" of the Sherlock Holmes tale. The fangs of rattlesnakes are fragile and sometimes snap off, but they are replaced by reserve fangs from at least six auxiliary teeth, so that rattlesnakes are always capable of delivering a fatal bite from the moment of birth until they die. And even after death, rattlers have been known to inflict a dangerous bite by means of their prolonged reflex action. The most elaborately toothed vipers have extra-long fangs that are curved like scythes and fold back when the mouth is closed. Of these monsters, the Gaboon viper has the longest fangs on record—deadly two-inch daggers that can penetrate muscles and arteries—and can come closer to delivering "instant death" than any other snake. The unique spitting cobra of Africa can project its venom up to 10 feet through the air, but it is harmless to humans unless it strikes the eyes, where it may have a blinding effect.

The Gila monster of the United States Southwest and its cousin the Mexican beaded lizard are the world's only poisonous lizards. Their venom is as toxic as that of snakes and can be fatal. Eight deaths have been recorded. The chances of encountering one of these rare and cumbersome creatures in the wild are slight and, of being bitten, slighter. Their venom comes from saliva glands in the lower jaw, and in order to deliver it they must spread it through the wound by chewing. Once they have gotten a grip, though, Gila monsters and beaded lizards hang on with bulldog tenacity, and sometimes it has been necessary to use pliers to separate one from a victim.

Among amphibians, a few salamanders and many frogs and toads excrete poisons that can kill animals as large as a dog. Several dozen South American frogs, however, present a potential threat to man, for their venom, extracted by Indian marksmen and used to tip blowgun darts, quickly kills animals.

Western rattlesnake

Rattles and Fangs

The most numerous and widespread poisonous snakes in the Americas are the rattlesnakes. Their range is continental, from Canada to Argentina, but only two species occur south of Mexico. Of the 30 species and 60 subspecies, the largest is the eastern diamondback, which may attain a length of more than eight feet, and the most notorious is the slightly smaller, extremely irritable western diamondback, which kills more people in the United States than all other poisonous snakes combined. Even so, the average is less than 14 people annually. The rattlers' unique trademark, the chain of rattles on their tails, are remnants of skin moltings. Baby rattlers are born with a button on the tip of their tails, and they add a new, hollow segment each time they shed their skin. The young semi-albino diamondback below, with its single rattle, has molted just once—a process that usually occurs within seven days of birth.

The widespread belief that a rattlesnake's age can be calculated by the number of rattles on its tail—one for each year of its life—is erroneous, since the snake may shed its skin and add a new podlike rattle three or four times a year. As a snake matures, the brittle tips of its rattle break off, leaving it with an average of eight or nine, like the timber rattlesnake above. One captive rattler, however, grew 27 rattles. Herpetologists are uncertain why the ominous-sounding rattles developed but theorize that the huge herds of large animals that roamed the western plains in prehistoric times trampled the snakes. The rattles evolved as a warning to them to stay clear.

As they are broken off, the hollow fangs of a rattlesnake are replaced by reserve fangs that grow in twin rows between the mature fangs, like those of the red rattlesnake at left. They are insurance that the snake will always be armed and able to secure food.

The water moccasin, or cottonmouth, is a native of the American South, a creature of swamps, lakes and streams. It spends its days in the water or on low-hanging bushes on the shore, lying in wait for the frogs, fish and other small creatures it feeds on. A portly snake, it sometimes reaches a length of five feet. When a cottonmouth opens its mouth before striking or as a warning (right) it reveals the stark white interior which gave it its common name.

Most of the native American venomous snakes are members of the pit-viper family, and the most prevalent are the rattlesnakes. The black-tailed rattlesnake at left is coiled in a striking position and has raised its rattles menacingly as a prelude to the furious rattling that, like the opening of the cottonmouth's mouth, is an instinctive threat gesture. Many other snakes which lack rattles also vibrate their tails as a warning.

The copperhead (left), like its close relative the cottonmouth, can deliver an extremely painful bite, but it is rarely fatal. Copperheads have clung tenaciously to their habitats and are still found near well-populated regions of the East Coast that have long since been deserted by rattlers and some other snakes. Their beautifully marked skins provide a marvelous camouflage, permitting copperheads to blend in almost invisibly with the leafy woodland floors where they live.

The elusive coral snake (on the left in the picture at right) is the most venomous of native U.S. snakes. It is sometimes confused with the harmless scarlet king snake (far right) and other brightly marked snakes. The formula for distinguishing between the lethal and the harmless: Coral snakes have black snouts and red, black and yellow, or red, black and white rings; the imitators have lighter snouts and yellow rings always bordered by black rings.

Thrills of a Naturalist's Quest

by Raymond L. Ditmars

Raymond L. Ditmars, who was Curator of Reptiles at the New York Zoological Society for many years, had a greater role than anyone in this century in introducing the public to the world of reptiles. His popular books and lectures helped cut away the myths and translate murky scientific research about reptiles, especially snakes, into terms that the layman could understand. Among his most popular books are Reptiles of the World *and* Snakes of the World. *In* Thrills of a Naturalist's Quest, *Dr. Ditmars describes the deadly fer-de-lance and an encounter he had with one in a Honduran rain forest.*

Walking around a turn in a tropical trail, I noticed a broken stump. It had formed the base of a big tree and stood a couple of feet high. The sides were firmer than the center and jagged, forming a margin for a nestlike area. The depression was filled with disintegrating wood of reddish color. Coiled precisely in the center was a snake. It appeared startling and incongruous—out of place in this peaceful forest. Yet its hues, like greenish velvet, harmonized with the surrounding tones. One might have stood right over it and not noticed it. It was realization that it was there; that in a split second it could change the observer's status from vigor to thought of death which made it appear so distinct.

This was my first meeting with the fer-de-lance in its domain. I have had various experiences in which it was concerned, both adventurous and scientific. A pair of these serpents, in the early days of my collection, had taught me to respect a lightning-like stroke, delivered without warning. . . .

Known under a number of Spanish and Portuguese names, it occurs throughout the low-lying coastal areas from southerly Mexico to the Argentine. In Central America it is called terciopélo (velvet snake) and barba amarilla (yellow beard). In Panama, in the Canal Zone, it is referred to as the "tommigoff," which doesn't mean anything in particular, but was picked up during the building of the Canal, sounded snappy, and has stuck. In South America it is called jararaca, owing to its javelin-shaped head. The name fer-de-lance originated among the Creole-French in the West Indies. While originally a local term, it has endured in reference to tropical wild life, although this serpent has largely disappeared from the islands where the name came into being, and relating to its head, in the form of an iron lance.

Unlike many poisonous serpents, this creature is rather slim and graceful. Usually it is around four feet long. Then there are sections where it grows to be eight feet long. I measured one in Honduras which was eight feet and four inches. At the thickest part it was not much over two inches in diameter. It was necessary to hold the creature by the neck, after pinning down its head. It seethed with rage and the jaws twisted sideways to bring the long, sharp fangs within reach of my fingers. The attendant, who stretched out the whipping length, and I gazed with awe upon those fangs. After we were done and had dropped the serpent in its cage we simultaneously heaved a sigh. . . .

What is the normal life of this creature, which can thus seethe with defensive fury, and so well realizes its possession of death-dealing mechanism? Surmise may point to it staining its trail with evil deeds. I have seen enough of it to know it is otherwise. It particularly fears man, and prepares for flight or defense in his presence. This might please the fundamentalists, if they sensed this enmity between serpent and man as I have broadly seen it in wide-flung parts of the world. They might apply such manifestation to biblical theory.

Accustomed to prowl and peer without frightening things, I have seen a slant of the so-called deadly snakes at variance with the general idea of their savagery. Undisturbed, and in environment remote from man, they are leisurely going, quiet creatures. On the floor of the tropic forests the fer-de-lance looks like a strip of softly tinted carpet. It glides in slightly undulated line, at times nearly straight, with the rate of progress of a man at a very slow walk. It can go much faster, but this is its natural gait. Its progress is uncanny. There appears to be no effort. The effect is of something pulled along, the body following declivities of the ground. For a moment the action appears explicable as the form moves down a slope. A stream of viscid fluid might follow such a course. But as the reptile progresses, it *ascends* a slope, and still there is no halting of the movement. It moves at the same speed as it seemed to flow down grade.

During this travel the head is often pointed to the ground. There is a quivering of forked tongue, which delicately touches the surface. This marvelous organ is searching for scent of prey, a rat, or fruit opossum. Picking up the scent by instantaneous taste, a type of sense which has come into being with serpents, the form goes on and into a thick tangle, which hides it. The tail disappears with that same effect of something being smoothly pulled forward.

Such a creature is capable of other actions of extreme delicacy. These attend the shedding of the skin. Two weeks before that event its lidless eyes start to bother it. At first they become dull and slightly bluish, like the eyes of some very old and senile thing. Their sight soon fails to the extent of seeing nothing more than a white veil, like peering into fog, and the serpent seeks a damp hiding place. The ideal spot is the depth of a hollow log, but if this cannot be found there is recourse to burrowing under a heap of forest débris. Here the thin outer garment becomes softened. The serpent emerges, looking much the same as it went in, but the eyes partially cleared again, the sign of its now being able to divest itself.

By turning the head sharply to one side, it rubs the top against an upstanding object. This is done with extreme care. The tissuelike integument is pushed from the top of the head, carrying the delicate eye plates with it. Attached to the skin, they are like lenses. The covering is pushed backward from the lower jaw. Then seeking an arching of stems through which it may slowly glide, and upon which the integument will catch, the serpent divests itself by moving forward and turning the old skin wrong-side out. Not a scale torn; no particle remains attached. The serpent glows like new velvet.

The Venomous Vipers

The venom apparatus of snakes reaches the height of development in the vipers of the Old World and the closely related pit vipers of the Americas and Asia. The slender fangs of these snakes consist of completely enclosed tubelike teeth through which the venom flows. The fangs are so long that they must fold back in the viper's mouth when not in use and are brought forward only when the snake is preparing to strike. The African bush viper (opposite, above) is a small, slim, arboreal viper. Most vipers are heavy, terrestrial snakes. The pit vipers, such as the bamboo viper (above) and the eyelash viper (opposite, below), are more advanced anatomically than the true vipers and have adapted to habitats that are usually unsuitable for their true viper cousins. Many have prehensile tails for life in the trees. The pit vipers derive their name from the two facial depressions located between the eye and the nostril. These are highly refined heat-sensing organs and serve as a sort of "sixth sense" to identify and locate prey.

The African bush viper (above) is the only true viper with a prehensile tail. It is less agile and moves more slowly than most other tree-living snakes, venomous or nonvenomous. Bush vipers feed primarily on tree frogs and small rodents and characteristically rest their heads on one tree branch while their tails are coiled around another, higher limb. The eyelash pit viper (left), which ranges from southern Mexico to Ecuador, is often found in a similar position. It is a nocturnal snake and gets its name from the series of little scales that protrude over its eyes.

The horned viper (right) can execute sidewinding motions over the sand, a trait common to desert-dwelling snakes. It is able to make an unnerving buzzing sound with its scales. The horned viper lives among desert shrubbery in Africa and Asia and is an excellent burrower. The sandy cover protects it from the sun during the day and helps keep the snake warm at night. The Russell's viper (below) is among the most deadly of the vipers and one of the most feared snakes of India, Burma and Thailand, for its half-inch fangs inflict deep, painful and deadly wounds. The potent venom of the Russell's viper is, however, the base for some medications used to promote coagulation of the blood.

The Gaboon viper (above), of the rain forests of eastern, central and western Africa, is the largest of all the vipers, with a heavy, plump body that may be as thick as a person's calf and up to six feet long. Although the Gaboon viper possesses spectacular two-inch fangs that contain a powerful venom, it is a generally lethargic animal that usually has to be excessively provoked or actually stepped on before it will bite.

Don't Tread on Me!

Although no snake preys on man, some of the poisonous ones do pose a threat to him. Among them is the mangrove snake (above) of Asia, Indonesia and the Philippines. This beautiful yellow-banded forest-dweller often reaches a length of eight feet. Although the bite of a mangrove snake is venomous, no known deaths have been attributed to it. The bite of an African mamba (photograph, opposite) is another matter; it can kill a man in 20 minutes. Attacks are quite rare, though, and usually occur when the snake is threatened and can find no escape route, for, like most poisonous snakes, the mamba will usually choose to flee rather than strike. Mambas are slender snakes that have the unusual ability to raise their bodies almost two feet off the ground while they race forward at speeds of up to seven miles per hour. They are most often found in treetops, where they feed on birds, lizards and rodents. The boomslang, seen chasing a bird in the film sequence (opposite), is generally docile by nature. But when it is seriously frightened or irritated, it inflates its neck, puffs out its body and strikes. A few human deaths, including that of the American herpetologist Karl P. Schmidt, have resulted from the boomslang's rear-fanged bite, but more often this African six-footer preys on the birds, frogs and lizards that share its arboreal home.

Rikki-tikki-tavi by Rudyard Kipling

Until Kipling wrote about Rikki-tikki-tavi in The Jungle Books *in 1894, most non-Oriental people thought a mongoose was some sort of bird. His classic tale of the spunky, chattering little snake-killer resulted in the wholesale importation of mongooses from India to Latin America, the West Indies and other areas of the world where poisonous snakes are a problem. But the alien mongooses proved a mixed blessing in their new environments, often ignoring the snakes they were supposed to kill and eating eggs and domestic animals instead. In the Kipling story, though, Rikki-tikki is a genuine hero. After adopting a British colonial family in India, he first kills Karait, a deadly krait, and then Nag, a cobra. The mongoose is in the act of destroying the cobra's eggs when a tailor bird tells him that Nagaina, Nag's mate, is threatening the family and sends Rikki-tikki scurrying toward the house.*

Rikki-tikki smashed two eggs, and tumbled backward down the melon-bed with the third egg in his mouth, and scuttled to the verandah as hard as he could put foot to the ground. Teddy and his mother and father were there at early breakfast; but Rikki-tikki saw that they were not eating anything. They sat stone-still, and their faces were white. Nagaina was coiled up on the matting by Teddy's chair, within easy striking-distance of Teddy's bare leg, and she was swaying to and fro singing a song of triumph.

"Son of the big man that killed Nag," she hissed, "stay still. I am not ready yet. Wait a little. Keep very still, all you three. If you move I strike, and if you do not move I strike. Oh, foolish people, who killed my Nag!"

Teddy's eyes were fixed on his father, and all his father could do was to whisper, "Sit still, Teddy. You mustn't move. Teddy, keep still."

Then Rikki-tikki came up and cried: "Turn round, Nagaina; turn and fight!"

"All in good time," said she, without moving her eyes. "I will settle my account with *you* presently. Look at your

friends, Rikki-tikki. They are still and white; they are afraid. They dare not move, and if you come a step nearer I strike."

"Look at your eggs," said Rikki-tikki, "in the melon-bed near the wall. Go and look, Nagaina."

The big snake turned half round, and saw the egg on the verandah. "Ah-h! Give it to me," she said.

Rikki-tikki put his paws one on each side of the egg, and his eyes were blood-red. "What price for a snake's egg? For a young cobra? For a young king-cobra? For the last—the very last of the brood? The ants are eating all the others down by the melon-bed."

Nagaina spun clear round, forgetting everything for the sake of the one egg; and Rikki-tikki saw Teddy's father shoot out a big hand, catch Teddy by the shoulder, and drag him across the little table with the tea-cups, safe and out of reach of Nagaina.

"Tricked! Tricked! Tricked! *Rikk-tck-tck!*" chuckled Rikki-tikki. "The boy is safe, and it was I—I—I that caught Nag by the hood last night in the bath-room." Then he began to jump up and down, all four feet together, his head close to the floor. "He threw me to and fro, but he could not shake me off. He was dead before the big man blew him in two. I did it! *Rikki-tikki-tck-tck!* Come then, Nagaina. Come and fight with me. You shall not be a widow long."

Nagaina saw that she had lost her chance of killing Teddy, and the egg lay between Rikki-tikki's paws. "Give me the egg, Rikki-tikki. Give me the last of my eggs, and I will go away and never come back," she said, lowering her hood.

"Yes, you will go away, and you will never come back; for you will go to the rubbish-heap with Nag. Fight, widow! The big man has gone for his gun! Fight!"

Rikki-tikki was bounding all round Nagaina, keeping just out of reach of her stroke, his little eyes like hot coals.

Nagaina gathered herself together, and flung out at him. Rikki-tikki jumped up and backward. Again and again and again she struck, and each time her head came with a whack on the matting of the verandah, and she gathered herself together like a watch-spring. Then Rikki-tikki danced in a circle to get behind her, and Nagaina spun round to keep her head to his head, so that the rustle of her tail on the matting sounded like dry leaves blown along by the wind.

He had forgotten the egg. It still lay on the verandah, and Nagaina came nearer and nearer to it, till at last, while Rikki-tikki was drawing breath, she caught it in her mouth, turned to the verandah steps, and flew like an arrow down the path, with Rikki-tikki behind her. When the cobra runs for her life, she goes like a whip-lash flicked across a horse's neck.

Rikki-tikki knew that he must catch her, or all the trouble would begin again. She headed straight for the

long grass by the thorn-bush, and as he was running Rikki-tikki heard Darzee still singing his foolish little song of triumph. But Darzee's wife was wiser. She flew off her nest as Nagaina came along, and flapped her wings about Nagaina's head. If Darzee had helped they might have turned her; but Nagaina only lowered her hood and went on. Still, the instant's delay brought Rikki-tikki up to her, and as she plunged into the rat-hole where she and Nag used to live, his little white teeth were clenched on her tail, and he went down with her—and very few mongooses, however wise and old they may be, care to follow a cobra into its hole. It was dark in the hole; and Rikki-tikki never knew when it might open out and give Nagaina room to turn and strike at him. He held on

savagely, and stuck out his feet to act as brakes on the dark slope of the hot, moist earth.

Then the grass by the mouth of the hole stopped waving, and Darzee said: "It is all over with Rikki-tikki! We must sing his death song. Valiant Rikki-tikki is dead! For Nagaina will surely kill him underground."

So he sang a very mournful song that he made up on the spur of the minute, and just as he got to the most touching part the grass quivered again, and Rikki-tikki, covered with dirt, dragged himself out of the hole leg by leg, licking his whiskers. Darzee stopped with a little shout. Rikki-tikki shook some of the dust out of his fur and sneezed. "It is all over," he said. "The widow will never come out again." And the red ants that live between the

then the steady *"Ding-dong-tock! Nag is dead—dong! Nagaina is dead! Ding-dong-tock!"* That set all the birds in the garden singing, and the frogs croaking; for Nag and Nagaina used to eat frogs as well as little birds.

When Rikki got to the house, Teddy and Teddy's mother (she still looked very white, for she had been fainting) and Teddy's father came out and almost cried over him; and that night he ate all that was given him till he could eat no more, and went to bed on Teddy's shoulder, where Teddy's mother saw him when she came to look late at night.

"He saved our lives and Teddy's life," she said to her husband. "Just think, he saved all our lives."

Rikki-tikki woke up with a jump, for all the mongooses are light sleepers.

"Oh, it's you," said he. "What are you bothering for? All the cobras are dead; and if they weren't, I'm here."

Rikki-tikki had a right to be proud of himself; but he did not grow too proud, and he kept that garden as a mongoose should keep it, with tooth and jump and spring and bite, till never a cobra dared show its head inside the walls.

grass stems heard him, and began to troop down one after another to see if he had spoken the truth.

Rikki-tikki curled himself up in the grass and slept where he was—slept and slept till it was late in the afternoon, for he had done a hard day's work.

"Now," he said, when he awoke, "I will go back to the house. Tell the Coppersmith, Darzee, and he will tell the garden that Nagaina is dead."

The Coppersmith is a bird who makes a noise exactly like the beating of a little hammer on a copper pot; and the reason he is always making it is because he is the town-crier to every Indian garden, and tells all the news to everybody who cares to listen. As Rikki-tikki went up the path, he heard his "attention" notes like a tiny dinner-gong; and

65

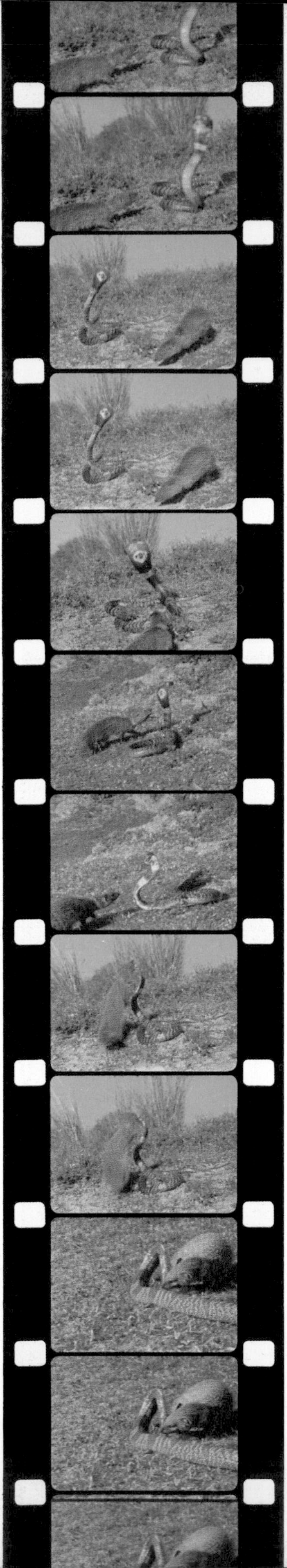

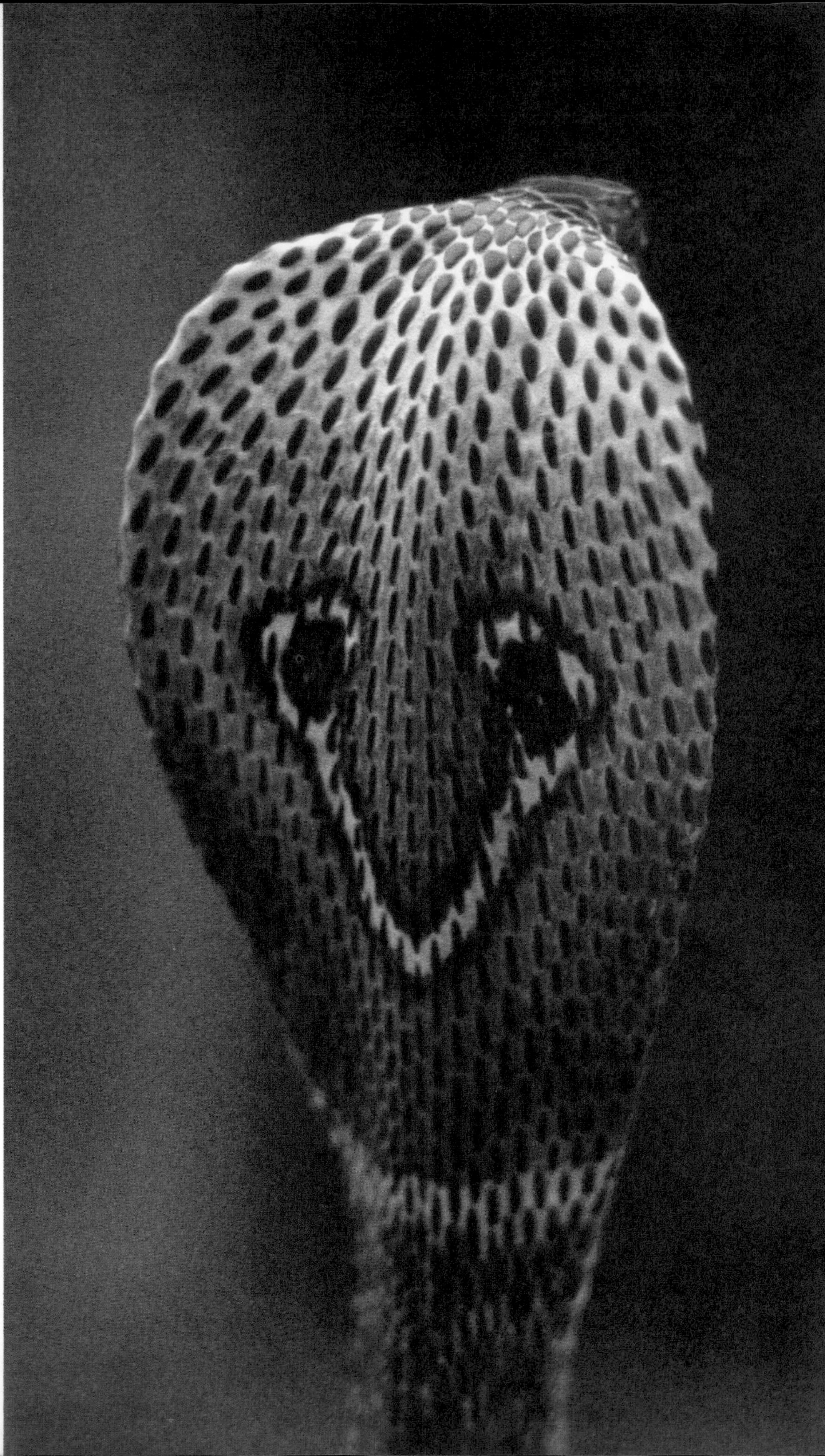

The Cobras: Hooded Menaces

The biggest of the venomous snakes is the 18-foot king cobra (right), whose head can be as large as a man's hand. The king cobra can deliver the most venom of all the snakes, and indeed its poison can kill an Asiatic elephant in three to four hours. But it is much less aggressive than smaller snakes, such as the Asian cobra, seen opposite and in the film sequence in which it is fighting a losing battle with a mongoose. This snake, with its distinctive black-and-white eyeglass marking, generally grows to a length of seven feet. It is the commonest of the species and is responsible for more human deaths than any other cobra. The eight-foot Egyptian cobra (below) is believed to be the deadly "asp" that killed Cleopatra.

Other Poisoners

Almost all amphibians secrete some poison through their skins, but the potency of the poison they produce varies greatly from species to species. The colorful poison-arrow frogs, like the four on this page, possess some of the most powerful toxin of all. Toxin from these tiny amphibians of the forests of South and Central America is collected by the local Indians, who then dip their blowgun darts in it. Small animals, such as birds or monkeys, wounded by these darts are immediately paralyzed.

Many lizards are accused of being venomous, but only the Gila monster (opposite) and the closely related beaded lizard deserve to be. Although a number of deaths have been attributed to Gila monster bites, their poison apparatus is less efficient than that of the poisonous snakes. The Gila monster's venom is contained in glands in the rear part of the lower jaw, some distance from the base of its fangs. Only vigorous chewing will make the venom flow along the membranes of the lizard's mouth and thus, finally, reach the victim.

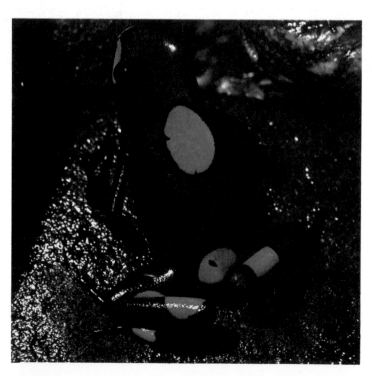

The slow-moving, desert-dwelling Gila monster (above) is a nocturnal animal that doesn't rely on vision but hunts by means of taste and smell. This lizard seeks out vulnerable prey such as nesting birds and rodents, newborn mammals or the eggs of birds and reptiles. But like all desert animals, the big lizard must be able to survive periods when food is scarce. During such times of famine the Gila monster is able to go for months without food, losing over 20 percent of its body weight, nourished only by the fats stored in its unusually thick tail, which becomes thinner as the nutrients are depleted.

Turtles

The timid, plodding tortoise has been the butt of jokes since the time of Aesop. And it *is* a comical reptile, with its burdensome shell, its awkward gait and its apparent stupidity. But turtles are not all awkward and slow; a pond turtle or even a giant sea turtle in its natural element is a creature of remarkable grace and speed. They apparently make use of celestial navigation: A box turtle, taken from its customary home range and deposited miles away, can find its way home—if it is a bright day. In cloudy or rainy weather, when the sun is invisible, it may become confused and lose its way. The sun or the stars may have some role in guiding the remarkable migrations every year of thousands of green sea turtles that leave their feeding grounds off the Cayman Islands to swim hundreds of miles across the Caribbean and deposit their eggs on the same beaches where they were born years before.

That clumsy-looking shell is actually a marvel of natural engineering and architecture. In the beginning of their evolution turtles were covered with scaly skin like other reptiles, but the scales eventually grew larger and into horny plates, and in the evolutionary process the plates fused together into carapaces, or upper shells, and plastrons, protecting the underbellies. These two shells were eventually joined at the turtle's sides, enclosing the animal in a bony armor, with holes for the feet, tail and head. Adjusting to its portable armor, the turtle's body was reorganized to comfortable dimensions and the shell became fused to the spine and some inner bone structure, leaving only the shoulder blades and the hip bones as movable joints. The turtle thus became the only land vertebrate in the world to wear part of its skeleton on the outside.

Early in the Mesazoic era turtles made certain refinements in their armor, adapting to their habitats. Those that returned to the water developed flattened, streamlined carapaces, and the claws of giant sea turtles evolved into flippers for easier navigation. Because they are more vulnerable to attack, the land turtles kept heavy, high-domed carapaces (opposite) and, in the case of the box turtles, hinged plastrons that enable them to retreat completely into the shell and snap shut. To carry those heavy turtle-ports around and to tear food apart, tortoises and pond turtles developed large, sturdy forelegs—webbed in the case of water turtles—and sharp claws.

Having achieved a design that inspired Roman legions to go into battle under a protective *Testudinaria*—a canopy of upheld shields sloped to resemble a turtle's carapace—and later military engineers to design the Sherman tank, turtles seem content with their Model T and have not evolved to fill as many environmental niches as their cousins, the lizards and snakes. They look pretty much today as their ancestors did 150 million years ago. They are considered to be an order in decline precisely because they have failed to change with the times, and today there are just over 250 identified species, divided into 10 families. They include strictly terrestrial tortoises, such as the box and Galápagos tortoises; semiaquatic turtles, such as the painted and spotted turtles; aquatic turtles, such as the snapping and soft-shelled turtles; and the giants of the sea, such as the leatherback and hawksbill turtles. In general, the term *turtle* applies to the whole order and to water and oceangoing turtles, *tortoise* to land turtles and *terrapin* to those freshwater turtles that are edible.

An extremely durable animal, the turtle is believed to be the longest-lived creature on earth. Some turtles, especially the large tortoises, may attain an age of 200 years.

Turtles and their eggs have long been a food staple in many parts of the world, and men have brought many varieties to the verge of extinction. For centuries it was the common practice for ships on long voyages to stop at islands with large turtle populations and take aboard hundreds of live tortoises as a source of fresh meat in the weeks and months ahead. The island of Rodriguez, lying in the Indian Ocean athwart one of the main sea lanes to the Orient, once supported a vast population of giant tortoises. "Sometimes you may see two or three hundred of them in a flock," wrote an early explorer in 1691, "so that one may go above a hundred paces on their backs . . . without setting foot on the ground." So popular were the tortoises as food for seafarers that by 1800 not a single one was left on Rodriguez. The Galápagos Islands' tortoises were almost extinct by the end of the 19th century. Similar depredations have reduced the population of green turtles, esteemed as a soup base, to the point of endangerment, and have threatened the diamondback terrapin, a delicacy from the Atlantic coast, the gopher turtle of the United States Southwest, a staple of Indian diets, and the river turtles of the Amazon and Orinoco river basins, slaughtered for their oily eggs and flesh. Even though conservationists have succeeded—through laws limiting harvests—in slowing the slaughter, these species are still slowly declining.

Radiated tortoises

The Ridleys' Riddle

The extraordinary homing instinct of sea turtles, like the Pacific ridleys pictured at right, has aroused the curiosity of such dissimilar groups as herpetologists and the United States Navy. What both would like to know, though for very different reasons, is how the ridleys navigate hundreds of miles of open ocean to find their way back to the very beaches on which they were born. For centuries the ridleys have made annual pilgrimages to the Costa Rican beach pictured here (there are seven such homing grounds known today—two beaches in Costa Rica and five in Mexico), swimming great distances to deposit their eggs in the sand at a mass nesting known as an *arribada*, or arrival. For many turtles it is their first contact with land since they were born. A female ridley may dig from three to five nests in the sand and leave as many as a hundred eggs in each. She returns to the sea after each nest of eggs is covered with sand, often copulating with the males that generally remain offshore (above), and ventures back the next day to leave more eggs to incubate in the warm sand.

In violation of the usual sea turtle precaution of nesting only at night, the ridleys (right) swarm across the beach in broad daylight to go about their nest-digging chores. There are thought to be three arribadas each year, occurring unpredictably from April to June. Once a female has chosen and cleared a nesting site, she digs with a furious display of sand-slinging that leaves her exhausted, barely able to drag herself back to the sea.

72

After excavating the nest entirely with her rear flippers, so that she never really sees what she is doing, the female ridley (above) deposits her eggs in the nest. Once the hatchlings emerge, they are able to reach the surface only through sibling teamwork, and even then their difficulties have just begun. How they locate the ocean from behind the dunes or debris near their nests is a mystery, though it is thought that they instinctively head for the brighter sky over the ocean.

74

The nests are emptied in a short time in a massive charge for the sea (left). To strike out singly would mean almost certain annihilation of the hatchlings. Even traveling en masse, few will reach their goal, and less than one percent will survive to adulthood. Ridley turtles may live for half a century in the open ocean, but their lives are never more threatened than in their first few minutes of existence. Of all the obstacles the hatchlings must contend with on their race to the sea—gulls, rock iguanas, ghost crabs and even the tropical heat, which their dark bodies absorb—none is a more skillful predator than the frigate bird (above). The frigate, which often feeds by catching flying fish in midair, is a relentlessly accurate hunter, and the hatchlings are not safe from it until they are in the water. Where the young turtles go when they do reach the ocean is yet another mystery. They begin what is called the "lost year," for where they live, what they eat and how they survive no one knows.

Soft-shelled Cousins

Some turtles, like the two pictured on these pages, have evolved without the horny plates that usually cover turtles' shells. The eastern spiny soft-shell (above) is a member of the world's most widespread genus of soft-shells, while the Fly River turtle (opposite) is one of the rarest of living turtles. The eastern spiny, named for the soft, pointed tubercles that rim the front of the adult's shell, grows to an average size of one foot. Like all soft-shells, it is nearly circular and almost flat and, as a result of this shape, shares with others of its species the epithet "flapjack" turtle. The eastern spiny inhabits the muddy or sandy bottoms of slow-moving rivers and is an extremely active, almost exclusively aquatic creature. Unlike other turtles, which have tough, cartilaginous beaks, the Fly River turtles have fleshy lips and a snout that is drawn into a proboscis, which they use as a snorkel. But the fleshy lips are deceptive, for hidden beneath them are strong mandibles capable of mangling a hand if these irascible turtles are disturbed.

The New Guinea Fly River turtle (below) might aptly be described as a "non-missing link," for although its shell is covered only by a layer of skin, as in the true soft-shell turtles, it has more in common skeletally with the non-soft-shells. Its shell is about 18 inches long, and its limbs have developed into paddles with only two claws (true soft-shells have three). The Fly River turtle, the sole surviving species of the family *Carettochelyidae*, inhabits the Fly River drainage basin in southern New Guinea. Although enough specimens have reached museums to make a complete description possible, almost nothing is known of its habits in nature, though it is recognized as a powerful swimmer. Recently it was discovered to have migrated to the Cape York region of northern Australia.

Turtle Necks

While there is some color differentiation between male and female turtles of the same species, it is not nearly so pronounced as the dramatic differences of fur and plumage that distinguish the sexes in many mammals and birds. Minor variations in head and neck patterns and eye color, for example, may occur among males and females of the same species. And it is true that male turtles generally grow darker as they mature, losing much of their coloring. The gallery of glowering grumps on these two pages represents seven fairly common American turtles and demonstrates that, their evolutionary conservatism notwithstanding, turtles come in a curious—and not always conservative—array of colors.

Top row, from left: One of the most familiar turtles, the eastern box turtle—so named because a hinge on the plastron permits the shell to be closed into a tight box—is a gentle, terrestrial creature whose range extends from New England to Florida. The common snapping turtle (center) is a vicious animal with a large, ungainly head and a long tail similar in shape to an alligator's. A primarily aquatic species, it is a voracious feeder that will eat practically any animal matter. The painted turtle (right) is often observed basking in large numbers on half-submerged logs. While it is found throughout most of the United States, it is the most common pond turtle in the northeastern states.

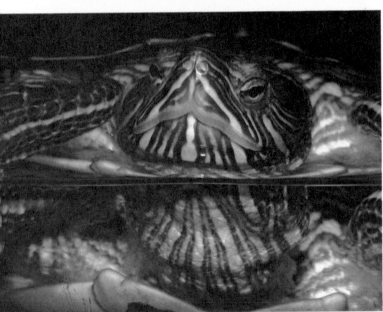
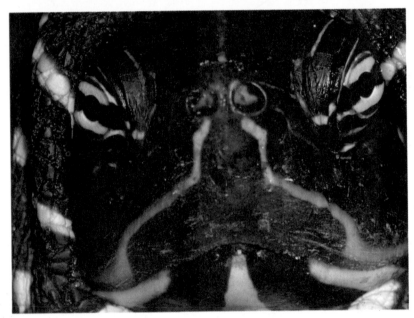

Bottom row, left to right: The peninsula cooter is a large, high-domed pond turtle whose carapace length may reach 15 inches. The wood turtle (second from left), one of the most terrestrial turtles in the Northeast, is a fast mover and a capable climber. Because of the loss of its habitat, it has become scarce and is now protected in New York State and other areas. The red-eared turtle (third from left) has been sold in dimestores for years. Such sales were recently banned in many areas when it was found to be a carrier of salmonella, an intestinal disease. The most characteristic feature of the chicken turtle (far right), so-called because of the chickenlike flavor of its flesh, is its unusually long, striped neck.

The Natural History and Antiquities of Selborne *by Gilbert White*

Gilbert White, a retired curate, observed the wildlife, geology and weather patterns of his native English village and the surrounding countryside. His recorded observations, The Natural History and Antiquities of Selborne, *published in 1789, has become a classic. Its literary excellence and scientific value are apparent in the following excerpt, which traces the life and life-style of one solemn, stately old English tortoise.*

April 12, 1772

On the first of November I remarked that the old tortoise, formerly mentioned, began first to dig the ground in order to the forming its hybennaculum [winter shelter], which it had fixed on just beside a great tuft of hepaticas. It scrapes out the ground with its fore-feet, and throws it up over its back with its hind; but the motion of its legs is ridiculously slow, little exceeding the hour-hand of a clock; and suitable to the composure of an animal said to be a whole month in performing one feat of copulation. Nothing can be more assiduous than this creature night and day in scooping the earth, and forcing its great body into the cavity; but as the noons of that season proved unusually warm and sunny, it was continually interrupted, and called forth by the heat in the middle of the day; and though I continued there till the thirteenth of November, yet the work remained unfinished. Harsher weather, and frosty mornings, would have quickened its operations. No part of its behavior ever struck me more than the extreme timidity it always expresses with regard to rain; for though it has a shell that would secure it against the wheel of a loaded cart, yet does it discover as much solicitude about rain as a lady dressed in all her best attire, shuffling away on the first sprinklings, and running its head up in a corner. If attended to, it becomes an excellent weather-glass; for as sure as it walks elate, and as it were on tiptoe, feeding with great earnestness in a morning, so sure will it rain before night. It is totally a diurnal animal, and never pretends to stir after it becomes dark. The tortoise, like other reptiles, has an arbitrary stomach as well as lungs; and can refrain from eating as well as breathing for a great part of the year. When first awakened it eats nothing; nor again in the autumn before it retires: through the height of the summer it feeds voraciously, devouring all the food that comes in its way. I was much taken with its sagacity in discerning those that do it kind offices: for as soon as the good old lady comes in sight who has waited on it for more than thirty years, it hobbles toward its benefactress with awkward alacrity; but remains inattentive to strangers. Thus not only "the ox knoweth his owner, and the ass his master's crib," but the most abject reptile and torpid of beings distinguishes the hand that feeds it, and is touched with the feelings of gratitude.

[Under December 9 we find this note:]

The old tortoise that I have mentioned in a former letter, still continues in this garden; and retired underground about the twentieth of November, and came out again for one day on the thirtieth: it lies now buried in a wet swampy border under a wall facing to the south, and is enveloped at present in mud and mire!

[Eight years later, under date of April 21, 1780, we read as follows:]

The old Sussex tortoise, that I have mentioned to you so often, is become my property. I dug it out of it's winter dormitory in March last, when it was enough awakened to express it's resentments by hissing; and, packing it in a box with earth, carried it eighty miles in post-chaises. The rattle and hurry of the journey so perfectly roused it that, when I turned it out on a border, it walked twice down to the bottom of my garden; however, in the evening, the weather being cold, it buried itself in the loose mould, and continues still concealed.

As it will be under my eye, I shall now have an opportunity of enlarging my observations on it's mode of life, and propensities; and perceive already that, towards the time of coming forth, it opens a breathing place in the ground near it's head, requiring, I conclude, a freer respiration as it becomes more alive. The creature not only goes under the earth from the middle of November to the middle of April, but sleeps a great part of the summer: for it goes to bed in the longest days at four in the afternoon, and often does not stir in the morning till late. Besides, it retires to rest for every shower, and does not move at all in wet days.

When one reflects on the state of this strange being, it is a matter of wonder to find that Providence should bestow such a profusion of days, such a seeming waste of longevity, on a reptile that appears to relish it so little as to squander more than two-thirds of it's existence in a joyless stupor, and be lost to all sensation for months together in the profoundest of slumbers.

While I was writing this letter, a moist and warm afternoon, with the thermometer at 50, brought forth troops of shell-snails; and, at the same juncture, the tortoise heaved up the mould and put out it's head: and the next morning came forth, as it were raised from the dead and walked about till four in the afternoon. This was a curious coincidence! a very amusing occurrence! to see such a similarity of feelings between both the shell-snail and the tortoise.

Because we call this creature an abject reptile, we are too apt to undervalue his abilities, and depreciate his powers of instinct. Yet he is, as Mr. Pope says of his lord,

"—*Much too wise to walk into a well:*"

and has so much discernment as not to fall down an haha, but to stop and withdraw from the brink with the readiest precaution.

Though he loves warm weather he avoids the hot sun; because his thick shell, when once heated, would, as the poet says of solid armour, "scald with safety." He therefore spends the more sultry hours under the umbrella of a large cabbage-leaf, or amidst the waving forests of an asparagus-bed.

But, as he avoids heat in the summer, so, in the decline of the year, he improves the faint autumnal beams, by getting within the reflection of a fruit-wall; and, though he never has read that planes inclining to the horizon receive a greater share of warmth, he inclines his shell, by tilting it against the wall, to collect and admit every feeble ray.

Pitiable seems the condition of this poor embarrassed reptile; to be cased in a suit of ponderous armour, which he cannot lay aside; to be imprisoned, as it were, within his own shell, must preclude, we should suppose, all activity and disposition for enterprise. Yet there is a season of the year (usually at the beginning of June) when his exertions are remarkable. He then walks on tiptoe, and is stirring by five in the morning; and, traversing the garden, examines every wicket and interstice in the fences, through which he will escape if possible; and often has eluded the care of the gardener, and wandered to some distant field. The motives that impell him to undertake these rambles seem to be of the amorous kind; his fancy then becomes intent on sexual attachments, which transports him beyond his usual gravity, and induces him to forget for a time his ordinary solemn deportment.

Lizards

The most successful and adaptable of all reptiles, lizards are found in every continent except Antarctica and have evolved into a fantastic variety of forms, colors and shapes. Lizards are at home in jungle treetops, burning deserts, rivers, tidelands, subarctic regions, grasslands—just about any habitat. They come in many sizes, from the tiny reef gecko, weighing a fraction of an ounce, to the 200-pound giant Komodo dragon of the Indonesian islands of Komodo and Flores. There are lizards like the *Draco*, or flying dragons, of Malaysia that glide through the air on winglike folds of skin and then furl themselves into something that resembles a shrunken leaf when they land on a tree. Other lizards, such as the "glass snake" and the blind worm lizards of the American West, have lost their legs through the course of evolution and are often mistaken for snakes or large worms. Some lizards can run erect on their hind feet, looking like miniature dinosaurs, and one—the green basilisk of Central America—can even scamper rapidly across the surface of water for short distances.

The ability to change color characterizes several lizards, notably the green anoles of the southeastern United States, sold as "chameleons" in circuses and pet stores, and the bizarre-looking true chameleons of Africa, Madagascar and Asia. Their repertory ranges from pale green to emerald to brown to gray and black. Both colors and patterns blend marvelously into whatever background they happen to encounter. But the master of color dynamics is the so-called bloodsucker of India, which gets its name from its habit of changing color during courtship or combat with rival males. It changes from a neutral brown to yellow, with cheeks, throat and neck turning a vivid scarlet. In other moods and situations the blushing bloodsucker—which does not suck blood at all but subsists on insects—can change itself into a whole rainbow of colors, from cinnamon-orange to jet black.

Only two lizards—the Gila monster of the southwestern United States (see page 69) and the Mexican beaded lizard—are venomous. The fat, lethargic Gila monster, with skin like Indian beadwork, has been captured and carried off to roadside menageries and individual collections in such numbers that the states of Arizona, California, Nevada, New Mexico and Utah have placed it under official protection to save it from extinction. Other large, nonvenomous lizards, such as the monitors and especially the Komodo dragon, are not known as man-killers but are quite capable of killing humans.

Most other lizards have neither poison nor great size as defenses and must rely on speed, camouflage or some special tricks to avoid predators. The portly chuckwalla of the southwestern United States and Mexico is able to inflate its body with air to twice its normal size. Under attack, it hides under a rocky ledge or in a crevice and inflates its body so that it is almost impossible to pull it out. But the Indians, who once savored the chickenlike flesh of the chuckwalla, learned to deflate the hapless creature with a pointed stick and drag it out. Chuckwallas, for their part, prefer flowers, and specifically brightly colored flowers, for food.

Skinks, which are common to all tropical and temperate regions of the earth, are among the most prolific families of lizards, with about 600 recognized species. With a few exceptions, they are recognizable by their glossy skins, and they run the gamut of lizard evolution, some with strong, well-developed legs, others with snakelike bodies and tiny, rudimentary limbs.

The majority of lizards are insectivorous and are important aids in keeping insect populations down. In tropical and subtropical countries the beautifully colored, large-eyed little geckos are welcomed into homes, where they relentlessly pursue flies, scorpions, mosquitoes and other pests. Endowed with remarkable fibrous footpads, geckos are able to scamper up a slippery wall or even across a ceiling on the trail of a fly.

The iguanids are one of the largest branches of the lizard tribe, ranging over the tropical and subtropical regions of the Americas and as far away as Madagascar and Fiji. They are a varied lot, remarkably adapted to their special environments. The rhinoceros iguana of Haiti (opposite) lives in an arid habitat, while the Galápagos marine iguana (overleaf) swims in the sea. The grotesque horned lizards—misnamed "horned toads"—look totally unlike their iguanid relatives, with flattened bodies and horny skin, an excellent desert camouflage and protection from predators. The horned lizard does resemble closely the Australian moloch, a completely unrelated lizard that evolved separately, halfway around the world, in an arid habitat that is almost identical to that of the horned lizard's—a perfect example of parallel evolution and of the versatility of the lizards.

Rhinoceros iguana

Oceangoing Lizards

Of all the lizards, only the marine iguanas of the Galápagos Islands (left and below) are true creatures of the sea. They are equipped with flattened, paddlelike tails that effortlessly propel their five-foot-long bodies through the water. The sea is the marine iguanas' source of food, providing the algae and seaweed these herbivores eat. Because of their specialized diet the lizards have developed special nasal glands through which they excrete the excess salt they ingest. But even with these nautical adaptations, marine iguanas spend most of their time on land, sunning themselves on the volcanic rocks that border the sea and feeding only at low tide. Mating also takes place on land and is often marked by outbursts of aggression among males defending and disputing their territories and the harems of females that gather around them.

Except at breeding time, marine iguanas are sociable animals. Herd members prefer to stay within 15 yards of shore, which often results in somewhat overcrowded conditions on the seaside cliffs (left). At low tide the lizards take to the sea (above), swimming easily, with only their dorsal crests and bumpy heads exposed.

Chromatic Chameleons

From their crested heads to their curling tails, chameleons are superbly constructed for life in the trees. Chameleons have opposable toes on all four feet, giving them firm footing on even the slimmest branches. Their usually long, thin tails are prehensile, providing a fifth grasping organ with which to climb slowly and steadily through their arboreal world. In addition, their unique eyes and tongue apparatus (see following pages) allow the lizards to zero in with deadly accuracy on the grasshoppers and other insects they love to eat. Chameleons also have the ability to alter the color and pattern of their skin. These changes are dictated by variations in temperature and light and especially by the lizard's "emotional" state. Thus, the same chameleon will look different in daylight from the way it looks at night, different when it attacks from when it is being attacked.

A remarkable number of species of chameleons, such as the delicately dappled creature on the opposite page, occur on the island of Madagascar. Like others of the family's 85 species, it furls its tail up tightly under its body when it is not in use. The majority of the chameleon family is found in Africa, like the so-called common chameleon at right. The few remaining species are native to southern Spain, southern India and Sri Lanka (Ceylon). This lizard has folded membranes or dewlaps at the back of its head that it spreads when excited or attacked, accounting for its other name, the flap-necked chameleon.

The African lizard below, called Meller's chameleon, is the largest chameleon outside Madagascar, having a tail and body length of up to 34 inches, four inches shorter than the largest species of the family, Oustalet's chameleon. Whereas most chameleons feed on grasshoppers, flies and worms, the Meller's chameleon, because of its size, requires either great numbers of insects or larger prey, like small mice and birds, to sate its appetite.

With tongues as long as their bodies, chameleons have been called the sharpshooters of the lizards. The hollow, unforked tongue of the Jackson's chameleon (above) is enlarged at the tip and covered with a sticky substance that adheres to the prey. A muscle contraction propels the tongue forward with amazing speed and precision. It is withdrawn with a second set of muscles and is kept bunched, like a pushed-up sleeve, in the lizard's mouth until it is needed again.

Acute vision is essential to the chameleon's survival, and, like the common African chameleon below, these lizards are equipped with eyes that are unequaled in the reptile world. Protruding like turrets from either side of the head, each eye is shielded by a thick eyelid that entirely covers the orb except for a small hole in the middle. With their unique capability of moving each eye separately or in coordination, chameleons are among the few animals with both independent and binocular vision. These organs are unrivaled in determining distances—a vital skill for this creature with its accurate, projecting tongue.

Whether they are defending their territories, threatening another creature or courting, anoles have a variety of ways of either attracting attention or camouflaging themselves. The Cuban knight anole (above), at 18 inches long, is the giant of the genus, but it looks even more formidable to foes and attractive to other anoles when it expands its azure dewlap and raises the scales that run along its back.

90

A Cast of Colorful Characters

Many lizards, in addition to the true chameleons, have the ability to change color. Among them are the anoles, such as the Cuban knight anole (opposite), which are often mistakenly called chameleons. Fast-moving forest-dwellers, they lack the true chameleons' prehensile tails and opposable toes. Instead anoles have five clawed fingers and toes on each limb which enable them to climb securely through the trees. The agama lizard (below) and the racerunner lizard (right) exhibit some dazzling color displays. Their scales are made up of cells that contain a dark pigment called melanin and droplets of colored oil. When the melanin is concentrated at the center of the cell, light is reflected through the oil from the small spot of melanin, determining the animals' light color. But when the lizard is under stress or when there are changes in temperature and light, the melanin expands, screening out the color reflected through the oil and giving the animal a darker appearance.

In many lizard families it is the male that exhibits the most beautiful color changes. The brightly striped racerunner lizard (above) of North and South America has a seasonal color repertoire. The males' coloring changes at breeding time and during disputes with other males over territory. The markings of the male agama lizard (left) of Africa and southwestern Asia are usually quite drab, but during the mating season he adopts the blue and purple blush that distinguishes him as a courting lizard.

The Sure-footed Geckos

Geckos are a family of quite remarkable lizards. They are relatively small animals, the largest of which, the tokay of Asia (left), is 15 inches long. Geckos are the vocalists of the lizard world, with well-developed voices ranging from subdued chirps to loud barks. Their feet usually end in enlarged toes that have lamellate, or scale-covered, soles (below). Most geckos are nocturnal animals—a factor in their ability to survive—with large, round, lidless eyes protected by a transparent membrane. These "contact lenses" are cleaned with a swipe of the lizards' tongue. Geckos' tails are autotomic and can be broken off at specific points by means of a muscle contraction. The wriggling of the discarded tail serves to distract an approaching enemy long enough to insure the gecko's escape and a new, shorter tail grows in its place. Geckos also have the ability to slough off their skins in times of danger. Almost all geckos have these characteristics in some modified form to help them survive in terrain as diverse as deserts and rain forests.

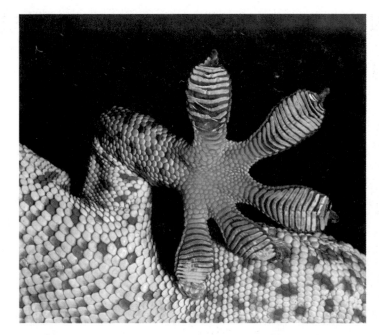

The Asiatic tokay, seen threatening an intruder above, is a plucky and persistent hunter, capable of subduing prey as large as a half-grown mouse. Like many other geckos, the tokay has scaled feet (right) lined with suction cups that are so tiny that they can adhere to the minutest irregularities on any smooth surface—even glass. The tokay moves by bending its broad toes backward, releasing the cups from the surface. With toes still flexed, it moves its foot to a new spot and presses the pads down again. When traversing rough terrain, such as the trunks of trees, geckos also employ the sharp claws at the tips of their toes.

The Miraculous Basilisks

The crested basilisk (above) is one of only four species of basilisks. A second is the green basilisk (below), running upright over water, a feat that it can duplicate on land as well. Basilisks' scaly feet move so quickly that they touch the water only briefly, barely breaking the surface.

Legend says that death comes to any living creature upon which the basilisk (a reptile said to be born from a cock's egg) fixes its gaze. The real basilisks, such as the crested (left) and the green (below), share nothing but their name with the mythical lizards. Basilisks are actually harmless members of the iguana family and are distinguished by tall crests along the backs of the males and scaly crowns on their heads, similar in appearance to the helmets in which their legendary namesakes were portrayed. The lizards range from southern Mexico to Ecuador, where they are usually found in shrubs near riverbanks. The shrubs and trees are sources for the small animals and fruits the basilisks feed on and serve as refuges from predators. Basilisks are not only good swimmers and divers; they are also capable of running swiftly, at speeds of over seven miles per hour, across the surface of water by hoisting themselves up on their long hind legs. Because of this remarkable ability to "walk on water," basilisks are known in some parts of their range as the Jesucristo lizards.

Bizarre Defenses

Lizards in general, and male lizards in particular, are combative animals. Disputes usually occur over territory, food or females and entail more bluffing than actual fighting. The bigger an animal, the more successful it will be in discouraging a rival. The frilled lizard (opposite) has large folds of skin around its head, which, when expanded, make it appear almost twice its actual size. The so-called flying dragon (above) has scaly, winglike membranes that extend like a cape from its front to its hind legs. At rest these broad flaps are folded against its body. But when searching for food or eluding a predator, the flying dragon unfurls its "wings," leaps from its high perch and glides gracefully, sometimes over a distance of 30 to 40 feet, to roost in another treetop. The sungazer lizard (left) is a 15-inch sun-lover from South Africa. It is the largest member of a family of club-tailed lizards that have large, spiny scales that encircle their tails and line their backs. Under attack, the sungazer defends itself by lying on its belly, arms and legs pulled close to its sides, leaving only its tough backside exposed. It clings tenaciously to the ground to avoid being turned onto its back and exposing its soft, unprotected belly.

The frilled lizard of Australia (above) gets its name from the collar of skin around its neck. The frill is covered with large, keeled scales and is supported by rods of cartilage. When courting or threatening, the lizard opens its mouth and erects its frill, which, in a 30-inch adult animal, can be as wide as 12 inches across.

Thermal Control

Reptiles' body temperatures are directly related to the temperature of their environment. In order to keep their bodies heated to the level at which they function best, reptiles must move to warmer or cooler locales to satisfy their heat requirements. Like all reptiles, the 18-inch chuckwalla (right) has no perspiration glands, which reduces its body's water loss to a minimum. Its scaly skin and low water excretion further help it to endure stifling heat, and it basks in the sun in temperatures that often soar to over 115° F. But during the chilly nights in its North American desert habitat the chuckwalla takes refuge in the relative warmth of a rocky crevice, the same retreat it seeks when it is being threatened or pursued.

The short-horned lizard (above) also does a disappearing act when it is under stress. This lizard's shovel-shaped head and flattened pancake shape help it to propel itself quickly under the sand, and its rapidly moving legs fling sand or dirt over its back to complete the covering. With only its head exposed, it is almost invisible but still able to keep a watchful eye on its surroundings. And when it is above ground, the short-horned lizard's iridescent coloring acts as a camouflage that blends in marvelously with the volcanic ash that covers its Arizona home.

The Tuatara

When European settlers arrived in New Zealand in the early 19th century they found a lizardlike animal that the native Maoris called tuatara, or "spine bearer," for the spiny crest that runs down its neck and back and gives it a rather noble appearance. The reptile had no commercial value, either for its olive, yellow-spotted, pebble-dash skin or as a food, and scientists at first dismissed it as just another member of the multifarious lizard order, possibly an iguana. Later investigations by herpetologists disclosed that the tuatara (opposite) was no ordinary lizard but a very special creature indeed, the unique descendant of an ancient order of reptiles that goes back to the Age of Dinosaurs and was thought to be extinct for 180 million years. Through millions of years the tuatara had apparently not changed and yet somehow managed to escape extirpation on its remote South Pacific island home. It was, in short, a "living fossil," a creature that had hardly changed in nearly 180 million years. In genus, family and order, the tuatara is the last, and only, creature of its kind. Just why the curious animal escaped the fate of the rest of the members of its order is a mystery.

By the time the tuatara was recognized as the one-of-a-kind survivor it is, man had nearly completed the job that time and nature had overlooked. By 1850 there were no more tuataras on the two main islands of New Zealand: The sheep, goats, rats and other animals the settlers brought with them had wiped them out. Today these prehistoric relics live on only in some 23 windswept islets off the northeastern coast of New Zealand's North Island and in the Cook Strait, between the two main islands. Some 10,000 survive in their island fastnesses; but, rigidly protected by the New Zealand government, they seem to be holding their own, except on six islands where Polynesian rats have been introduced and prey on young tuataras. But, barring some sudden environmental change, they should continue to live.

Their survival depends completely on an undisturbed way of life. The tuatara shares its islands with swarms of seabirds. The birds live in burrows, and tuataras, though perfectly capable of digging their own holes, often move in with the birds. The rooming arrangements are usually amiable, although the primitive reptiles will sometimes eat the birds' eggs or nestlings or drive the original burrowers away. They seem to be loners, often grumpy by nature. The seabirds will occasionally eat a young tuatara. Perhaps as a natural means of self-preservation, tuataras are nocturnal, emerging from their holes at dusk, when the birds are in their burrows. Tuataras hunt the large, wingless crickets known as wetas, as well as the beetles, snails and geckos that are their principal food.

Tuataras differ uniquely from lizards and other reptiles in the structure of their skulls and bones. Another distinctive characteristic is a third eyelid, a translucent "window wiper" that sweeps across the surface of the lens from the inner corner while the two conventional eyelids are open. A third, or "parietal," eye is socketed in the top of the tuatara's head, clearly visible in younger animals but covered over with thickening skin as the tuatara ages. The third eye is unable to perceive images but is sensitive to heat and light and probably functions as a kind of thermostat, alerting the tuatara to get out of the hot sunlight. Tuataras have a much greater functional ability in cold weather than other reptiles. They are active when the temperatures are as low as 45 degrees F. but are most comfortable when the reading is about 52 degrees.

Adult male tuataras weigh over two pounds and grow to a length of more than two feet; females are slightly smaller. In the New Zealand summer (November to February) the female lays a clutch of eight to 15 parchment-shelled eggs in a shallow hole, usually some distance from her own burrow, on a sun-warmed hillside. The eggs do not hatch for 13 to 15 months, the longest incubation period of any reptile, although they are ready to hatch by the beginning of the second summer. Instead, they go through a period of aestivation (summer dormancy) for several months before the young tuataras break out of their shells. Neither parent pays the slightest attention to the young, and the babies are on their own from birth.

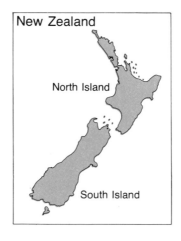

The tuatara formerly ranged over both main islands of New Zealand (green) but has been reduced to a sprinkling of offshore islets (red).

98

Crocodilians

The closest surviving relatives of the dinosaurs, crocodiles are descended from a common ancestor of the great extinct beasts. They are also the prototype of the mythical dragon, and in parts of India and Africa they are venerated as surrogates and high priests of the gods. During prehistoric times monster crocs, measuring more than 50 feet from their menacing snouts to the tips of their tails, roamed the swamps and lakes, but they passed into extinction at the end of the Age of Reptiles. Surviving members of the order grow to approximately half that size—a 27-foot saltwater crocodile is the absolute record—and dwindle downward to the African dwarf crocodile, which measures little more than three feet. Even so, pound for pound, the crocodiles are the largest reptiles.

Crocodilians, along with turtles and the tuatara, are so-called conservative animals that have changed very little in the past 150 million years and have been content to go on occupying the same watery environments they lived in during the Paleocene era. Perhaps because of their slow rate of evolution all that remain today are three groups—the crocodiles of Africa, Asia and the Americas; the alligators of the southern United States (opposite) and China and the caimans of Latin America; and the lone gharial of southern Asia. All have long snouts with formidable rows of teeth, thick-plated armor that would delight a medieval knight, waterproof flaps over their ears and special respiratory systems that enable them to eat while submerged without breathing water into their lungs. The differences between the three kinds are slight: Crocodiles have narrower snouts and some protruding teeth; alligators and caimans have wider snouts and tucked-in teeth; and gharials are equipped with almost ridiculously long and narrow jaws containing large numbers of extremely sharp teeth that allow quick side-to-side foraging as they pass through schools of fish. All live in fresh or brackish water except for the saltwater crocodile, which prefers seacoasts and river mouths and will readily take to the open sea, swimming as far as 1,000 miles from the nearest land.

The family's reputation as vicious killers is not well earned. A few species will attack animals as large as small giraffes, young hippopotamuses and giant anacondas. All are carnivorous, and some are cannibalistic and will unhesitatingly devour their own young. For this reason young crocs are rarely seen around the haunts of their elders after they leave their mothers' protection. After a few years in prudent seclusion, when they have grown big enough to protect themselves, they reappear. Adult males preside over territories and characteristically bellow to attract females and proclaim their territorial boundaries. During the breeding season the males lie offshore like patrol boats while harems bask, jaws agape, in the sun.

The female crocodiles are remarkable mothers. They deposit their eggs in cone-shaped mounds or foot-deep holes in the sand which they laboriously build and shape for as long as three or four days. After the eggs are laid, the mothers keep an almost constant vigil nearby to ward off mongooses, monitor lizards or other egg-fanciers. Some birds nest in the vicinity so that their eggs will also be protected by the watchful mother crocs. When the baby crocodilians are ready to hatch, after an 11- to 14-week incubation period, they announce it from within their shells, 10 or more inches deep, in audible peeping sounds that have been described as like the contented noises puppies make when they nurse. Then the mother crocodile or alligator carefully uncovers them—they could not possibly dig their own way out—and gently takes the squirming 10-inch babies, three or four at a time, in her grinning mouth, to the water's edge. For the next few weeks the young crocs swim after their mother like baby ducks, crawling over her face and back and taking refuge at night in rushes and under rock ledges. Soon thereafter they go into their disappearing act.

If the crocodilians are an occasional menace to mankind, their own wanton slaughter by man is comparable to the destruction of the bison or the passenger pigeon. Untold millions of crocodilians have been turned into shoes and handbags for their durable and beautifully grained hides.

As the populations, the annual harvests and the size of the hides inevitably declined, conservation groups at last succeeded in getting some laws passed to save the survivors. But the insatiable demands of the fashion market persist, and poachers have moved in. When crocodilians' skin was banned in New York and other states, there were ready markets for it in France and Japan. Game preserves and "farms" where hatchlings are protected and raised under vigilant guard have been of some help, and there are some hopeful signs of a revival of the American alligator in the nine Southern states where it is protected. But unless some stringent international taboo on the uncontrolled slaughter can be enforced, the crocodilians may soon be no more than the grin on their fossil bones as they join those monstrous ancestors in oblivion.

American alligator

The Birth of a Baby Croc

Crocodilians are territorial animals. Each male presides over an area in the water and a harem of females gathers around him. Courtship between crocodilians, such as the American alligators at left, takes place in the water. So does copulation, with the male holding the female with his front feet. All crocodilians are egg-layers. Some, like the Nile crocodile seen below carrying a soon-to-be-hatched egg in her mouth, dig nest holes in sandy riverbanks. Nest holes most exposed to the sun are the deepest, sometimes 20 inches deep. Once the nest is ready the female lays as many as 40 or more white, hard-shelled eggs and covers them with soil and grass. Other crocodilians, such as the American alligator, build mounds of fermenting swamp vegetation in which to incubate their eggs. The eggs are buried and the heat created by the decomposition of the vegetation promotes their development. The female guards her eggs until they are ready to hatch, a process that, depending on the species, can take as long as 14 weeks. She leaves her post only when the heat becomes unbearable and she is forced to take a swim.

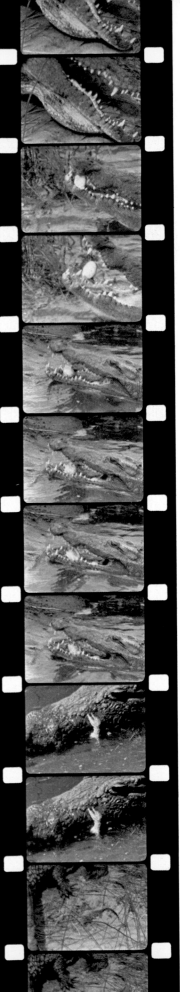

Hatching time for the young crocodilians, like the crocodile baby above, is heralded by the squeaking noises coming from beneath the nest covering. As their mother unearths the eggs with her feet, the newborn reptiles break through their shells by means of their egg tooth—a horny growth protruding from the top of their snouts. If, as in the film sequence at right, the baby crocs are unable to crack their shells, they are gently aided by their mother, who carefully carries the eggs to the water before helping her babies gain their release.

Caimans, Gharials and Gators

Although they are amphibious reptiles, crocodilians, such as the American alligator (right), the South American caiman (below) and the Indian gharial (opposite, below), are better suited for life in water than on land. They mate, hunt for food and swim in the water. The crocodilians' ears and noses are waterproofed with special valves that close when the animal is submerged. Their eyes are protected by well-developed upper and lower lids as well as by a third, transparent shield.

Crocodilians come on land to build their nests, lay their eggs or to sun themselves. During the blistering heat of midday they usually lie motionless on spits of land with their mouths wide open, allowing the moisture from their oral membranes to evaporate. But when the heat becomes too intense they must return to the water to cool the rest of their body. When disturbed, they are capable of raising themselves up on their stubby legs and moving at a surprising speed, but only over short distances.

The jacare of Paraguay (left) is one of the four so-called spectacled caimans of South America, named for the bony ridge between its eyes that resembles the nose bridge on a pair of eyeglasses. A denizen of slow-moving streams and bayous, the jacare feeds mainly on giant water snails of the Paraguay River.

Like all crocodilians and most aquatic animals that stay primarily on the surface of the water, the American alligator's nostrils, eyes and ears are on one plane on the top of its head (left). This permits the animal to breathe, see and hear and still remain nearly submerged and virtually unseen. The Indian gharial, sometimes called gavial (below), is the only crocodilian with teeth that are of a nearly uniform size and form. Like its relatives, the gharial uses its teeth for seizing and holding fish prey, not for chewing it.

Caecilians

In 1920, during a specimen-collecting expedition to the Philippine island of Basilan, Edward H. Taylor, the American herpetologist, found a legless, wriggling creature underneath a log. After a perfunctory inspection he decided that it was just another earthworm and dropped it on the ground. To his surprise, the animal moved off, not in the characteristic concertina fashion of worms but in a very deliberate, serpentine wriggle, exactly like a slow-moving snake. Picking it up again, he examined the animal more closely and decided that he had discovered neither a snake nor a worm but a hitherto unknown species of caecilian. And what, one may properly ask, is a caecilian? It is not a native of Sicily but "the worm with a backbone," one of the least-known vertebrates on earth. Many herpetologists know it only from books and pictures, and only a few thoroughgoing scientific studies of caecilians have been made. Most laymen have never heard of the animal. And yet it is one of three surviving orders of amphibians that have lived on the earth longer than any other land creatures, the cousin of the familiar frogs and salamanders.

Physically, caecilians cannot be called handsome creatures. Their size ranges from four inches to four and one half feet and their color varies from charcoal-gray to pink. Their elongated bodies are segmented in circular or semicircular folds called annuli, but these have no function in moving, as the segments of an inchworm or a caterpillar do. They are the only amphibians that have a scattering of rudimentary scales. Although a few species are aquatic, most caecilians spend their lives in burrows in moist ground and under leaves, rocks, rotten logs and debris, searching for the worms and insects they feed on. They venture out on the surface of the ground at night, but the slightest glimmer of light drives them back to the darkness of their subterranean world.

Because they live in darkness, adult caecilians have little or no need for vision, and as a consequence their eyes are either very small and almost functionless or even overgrown by skin. Their sense of hearing is not very keen, either, and caecilians rely instead on small moving feelers or tentacles that sprout from their heads, near the eyes or nostrils, as they grow to adulthood, and on an excellent sense of smell. One African species has eyes on the tips of the tentacles. Their heads are important as burrowing instruments, so caecilian skulls are heavily boned and compact, and their muzzles often protrude belligerently. Although all caecilians have teeth, few are harmful to anything larger than a beetle or grub. The Indians of the Oax-

aca region of Mexico are unconvinced, though. They firmly believe that the metlopils, or Lafrentz caecilians, which they sometimes turn up with their plows are deadly poisonous and savage biters, and they give them a wide berth.

There are over 150 recognized species of caecilians, in four families, located in tropical and subtropical parts of the Americas, Africa, Asia and the Indonesian and Philippine archipelagoes.

Herpetologists believe that there are many undiscovered species of caecilians in areas of Sumatra and South America that have been poorly explored or unexplored zoologically. Those species that are known are still being named and classified, and there is much disagreement among herpetologists about their descriptions and characteristics. Until 1879 caecilians were classified as reptiles, described as a separate order of "pseudosnakes."

Courting almost certainly takes place when the caecilians come to the surface of the ground in the darkness of night; the breeding seasons are after the annual monsoons, or rainy seasons. Though most caecilians are oviparous, six species give birth to live young, small replicas of their parents that are nursed through the larval stage within the mother's body with a special uterine milk.

Egg-laying caecilians usually produce a clutch of about two dozen eggs, which they gather together in bunches in damp burrows near running streams. During incubation the mothers coil protectively around the eggs to guard them from burrowing snakes and legless lizards, which, because of their ability to follow them into their burrows, are the caecilians' principal enemies. As they incubate the eggs become annealed together and gradually absorb water from the damp earth, until they double in size. When they hatch, young caecilians are four times as large as the newly laid eggs.

Hatchlings have frilly, scarlet external gills, which they quickly lose. They go, nevertheless, to the water near their birthplace and begin a lengthy aquatic stage before metamorphosing into strictly terrestrial adults. During their watery larval phase young caecilians have large eyes and a tailfin, which gradually deteriorate as their tentacles develop and their skin changes texture. Nineteen aquatic caecilians of South America have only one functional lung; all others become bound to the land in adulthood. However, like all amphibians, they require considerable moisture in order to survive in their forest or riverbank habitats. They are, in fact, so completely terrestrial that if they are forced to stay in the water, they drown.

Salamanders

The term *salamander* comes from a Greek word meaning "fire animal"; the association of the aquatic creature with fire is part of an ancient myth. In medieval times, when men brought wood into their houses and stacked it by their hearths, salamanders often crawled from the bark and ran around, giving rise to the belief that they were impervious to fire, so cold-blooded indeed that their bodies could extinguish the flames. They are, of course, as susceptible to fire as any other animal and cannot tolerate heat.

Another widely held myth about salamanders—that they are deadly poisonous—comes closer to the truth. Some salamanders emit poisonous secretions that can kill small predators and can cause a searing pain when accidentally rubbed into human eyes but are otherwise harmless to man. Such poisoners as the red eft, with its gaudy orange-red coat, go about quite boldly, apparently aware that would-be predators will instinctively avoid them.

Many salamanders are often confused with lizards, although the differences that distinguish them are profound. True amphibians, most salamanders spend at least part of their lives in fresh water and usually undergo a metamorphosis when they lose their gills and become terrestrial animals. They do not have scales to protect their bodies as lizards do, and their naked bodies require water or a constant high humidity level all of their lives. Lizards characteristically have five clawed toes on each limb; salamanders have no claws and never more than four toes on their front legs.

Salamanders are found in most parts of the world, in a surprising variety of habitats. Several kinds of blind salamanders live out their lives in total darkness in underground streams and caves. There are salamanders that live in trees and newts that never leave the water. The fire salamander of Europe, on the other hand, is such a completely terrestrial creature that it sometimes drowns when it returns to the water to mate. In 1865 a pair of Mexican axolotls in the Jardin des Plantes in Paris caused a scientific sensation when they unexpectedly mated and produced a brood that divided into two groups. Several of the young lost their gills, left the water and were identified as the familiar tiger salamanders, while others of the same brood remained aquatic larvae all their lives. The perplexed scientists who observed this unusual behavior first decided that the axolotl (opposite) was a rare example of counter-evolution, a species in the process of reversion to its original, entirely aquatic state. Later the axolotl and the tiger salamander were recognized as separate but closely related species that can retain their gills as an adaptation to a totally aquatic life.

The terms *eft* and *newt* are old Anglo-Saxon words meaning "lizardlike." While they are used interchangeably to describe many salamanders, the eft is, strictly speaking, the animal in its land cycle, and the newt is the animal in its watery phase of life. Thus, the red-spotted newt becomes the red eft when it loses its gills and olive-green, red-speckled swimming colors and assumes its bright red coat for the two or three years it spends as a strictly terrestrial creature. It becomes a red-spotted newt again when it returns to the water for the rest of its life.

Salamanders usually change their color and appearance, often dramatically, when they emerge from the water. Some undergo further changes at other stages of their lives. When mating, the male crested newt of Europe sprouts a serrated "nuptial crest" on its head and back, giving it the appearance of a miniature dragon. The rare grotto salamander is born with eyes, but during metamorphosis, when it enters the dark cave where it will spend its life, its eyelids grow together and it becomes blind. The Georgia blind salamander, one of the rarest of all salamanders, is completely eyeless.

Not much is known about the breeding habits of most salamanders. Some, like the crested newt, have complicated courting rites and dances. Most are egg-layers, depositing their eggs in streams or ponds in gelatinous strings like beads, with each egg in a single, round packet. In one American lungless species some females retire to a hole or under a rock, lay their eggs together in a mass, like tiny toy balloons, and guard them until they hatch.

Most salamanders are secretive and solitary animals and are rarely seen. Though loners, they do live in the same neighborhood and often hibernate together or gather in large groups for the annual migration—often over considerable distances—to the trysting pools where they breed. In Heidelberg and the Hartz Mountains of Germany there are large populations of fire salamanders, which are rarely seen. But after a drenching rainstorm in the summer or early autumn they suddenly appear, thousands of them, slipping through the leaves in search of earthworms and insects. Their sudden appearance, as if they had actually fallen from the skies with the rain, may have something to do with the salamander's reputation as a creature of mystery and magic.

Mexican axolotl

Newts and Efts

Of the 2,800 species of amphibians that exist today, 285 are salamanders. Many salamanders begin their lives in the water. A few remain aquatic and others become arboreal, but the great majority develop into ground-dwellers. Even during the terrestrial part of their lives salamanders are dependent on moisture for their survival. Their smooth, porous skin offers them little protection against dehydration. And because they are unable to drink, salamanders must get their water from their environment. In dry weather these usually shy creatures burrow into subterranean recesses, often spending months below ground searching for food and moisture. Many, like the ringed salamander at left, are nocturnal and come out during the day only when it is raining. Others, like the red-spotted newt seen below in its land, or red eft, stage, stay terrestrial for a two- or three-year period and then return to the water to become permanently aquatic, lung-breathing adults.

The salamander at left, called Pseudoeurycea belli, is one of the most distinctive salamanders in Mexico and also one of the largest, growing to a length of over eight inches. Many Pseudoeurycea salamanders, of which there are about 22 species, inhabit the central Mexican plateau. Most·are terrestrial animals, but some are accomplished climbers as well.

The California newt (right) is usually found in ponds along the western coast of the United States. It is forced to live on land during the hot summer months when the ponds dry up. The breeding season begins when the winter rains replenish the ponds. California newts are born in the water, but as soon as they lose their gills, through the process of metamorphosis, they come on land. They would drown if compelled to stay in the water.

Frogs and Toads

Caecilians are sometimes mistaken for worms or snakes, and salamanders may be confused with lizards, but members of the third surviving order of amphibians—frogs and toads—are unmistakable. Tailless, with bulging eyes and big grinning mouths, the families of frogs and toads are unique. And they proclaim their singularity: No one who has ever heard the spring peepers' annual ovation to love or the bullfrog's booming "jug-o-rum" on a summer night can confuse the noisy creatures with any other animal. Like songbirds, each species has its own distinctive vocalization and can be identified by the sound it makes.

Frogs are generally semiaquatic, web-footed, with naked, clammy skins and powerful hind legs that enable them to jump astonishing distances and are, unfortunately for frogs, esteemed by gourmets for their tasty, chickenlike thighs. Toads are terrestrial, homely and often covered with wartlike bumps that exude poisonous fluids. They lack the vaulting legs of frogs and move in short, rapid hops. And if frogs are sought after for their legs, toads are valued as nonpareil destroyers of insects. In France, toads are sold commercially, to be released in gardens as natural pesticides. Apart from their value as food or insectivores, frogs and toads are among the most widely used laboratory animals. *Xenopus*—a pipid, or clawed, frog—was used for the first reliable pregnancy test in humans.

Almost all toads and frogs of temperate North American habitats lay eggs in the water in the spring, in gelatinous masses or strings, and usually in prodigious numbers. The common American toad may lay as many as 30,000 eggs, in long strings trailing far behind them. The great numbers are a form of insurance for survival, for the tiny tadpoles are fair game for turtles, fish, birds and other predators, including other frogs. Spadefoot tadpoles even eat each other when food is scarce.

While they are cannibals, frogs do not seem to go after their young deliberately. Instead, they apparently have a vague guiding principle when it comes to size: If a moving figure is smaller, eat it; if it is the same size, mate—or attempt to mate—with it; if it is bigger, flee from it. This simple reaction can sometimes be fatal, for if a frog attempts to attack or mate with a frog of another species, a common occurrence, it may be fatally poisoned. The pickerel frog of North America exudes a defense poison that kills other species of frog on contact.

The breeding habits of toads and frogs are closely controlled by the weather. A sudden cold spell in early spring will silence the peepers' mating choruses until the temperature warms up again. Other frogs, creatures of the Arctic tundra or Alpine lakes, breed only in the early spring, when the weather is still cold, to allow for maturation of the tadpoles during the very short summer. Spadefoot toads will mate only after a raging rainstorm, when the temperature is 50 degrees or higher. If there are no heavy rains in a breeding season, there will be no new spadefoots that year. But when conditions are right, spadefoots emerge from their burrows and spawn with the speed of lightning. The eggs are deposited in fast-evaporating puddles or rainpools, hatch into tadpoles in a day and a half and complete their metamorphosis into little toads in 11 to 12 days. Some species, notably the greenhouse frogs of the southeastern United States, skip the tadpole stage altogether and are hatched as tiny froglets. And one African toad is unique, giving birth to live young.

There are some kinds of frogs and toads that make remarkably good mothers and fathers. The male midwife toad of Europe wraps his mate's eggs around his legs, carrying them to their watery hatcheries. The female Goeldi tree frog of Brazil carries the eggs in the hollow of her back. Most curious of all is the male Darwin's frog, native to some Chilean islands, which appears to swallow his mate's eggs when they are about to hatch, then carries the tadpoles in his capacious vocal sac for 15 to 20 days before spitting them out into watery nurseries.

Frogs and toads have a wide range of sizes, from the half-inch Cuban poison-arrow frog, tiniest of all amphibians, to the 14-inch Goliath frog of Zaire, and Blomberg's toad, which grows to 10 inches and lives in the rain forests of Colombia. A few frogs, like the horned frogs of South America (opposite), can bite painfully, and the gaily decorated little strawberry frog and related species of Central and South America secrete a poison from their glands which, when applied to blowgun darts, will cause death in small animals and birds in minutes (see page 68). In general, frogs and toads are amiable and useful animals that have never been known to kill or seriously hurt a man. In Malaysia, indeed, one vividly colored frog has been canonized in the local religion and is carried about on a special throne on holy days. Despite such occasional veneration, though, there is no recorded instance of a frog that will turn into a prince when it is kissed.

South American horned frog

Eggs Galore

Adult frogs lead almost exclusively terrestrial lives, but for mating and egg-laying they usually return to the water. Mating, which takes place accompanied by the loud croaking of the male, is fairly similar among these amphibians. Like these European frogs (left), the male lies across the female's back and grasps her under her arms. As the clusters of eggs are ejected from the female they are fertilized by the male. The places in which frogs customarily lay their eggs differ from species to species. Some eggs, like those of the bullfrog (below) and the green frog (opposite, below), are often deposited among aquatic plants. Others, like those of the tree frog (opposite, above), are laid in the forked branches of a tree overhanging a pond or stream. Then there are certain frog mothers and fathers that carry their eggs imbedded in their backs or wrapped around their legs. Other, less devoted amphibian parents leave their eggs floating in the open water, where the bubbly masses are preyed upon by fish, birds and even tadpoles.

The eggs of a South African tree frog (left) hang like a Christmas ornament from a tree near the water's edge. As tadpoles develop within the eggs, they break through their gelatinous capsules and fall into the water, where they remain until they have undergone metamorphosis. (For a detailed explanation of metamorphosis, see overleaf.) The numerous eggs of the African green frog (below) seem to fill the stream where they incubate. It is estimated that every female frog lays a staggering 5,000 eggs per season. But because only two or three of these will reach adulthood, the total number of frogs in the world is gradually diminishing.

The Magic of Metamorphosis

This sequence of pictures shows the development of the European frog from a newly laid egg (1) to a completely metamorphosed frog. The transformation usually takes from two to three months but varies with the temperature of the water and the availability of food. The newly hatched tadpoles (2) cling to their egg envelopes with fibers that grow from the area where their mouths will ultimately develop. When they are a few days old the tadpoles have antlerlike external gills (3). They also develop functional eyes, and the tail, with its rudderlike crest, becomes apparent. At two to three weeks (4) the tadpoles are breathing by means of internal gills and are feeding primarily on plants. The hind legs appear after about seven weeks (5) and the front legs some two weeks later (6). By the time the internal gills have degenerated, replaced by lungs, and the tail has shrunk to a mere stump, the 10-week-old frog (7), now more than half an inch long, is ready to leave the water.

1

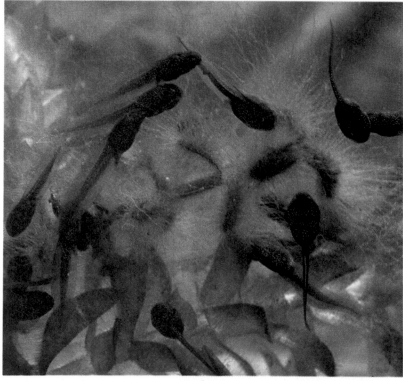

4

5

2

3

6

7

118

Frogs in Fancy Dress

The words "frog" or "toad" usually conjure up visions of an olive-drab bullfrog or a warty common toad. Actually, the order has as many bizarrely marked and vividly colored species as any in the animal kingdom. With some species, like the poison-arrow frogs of Latin America, the gaudy markings are warnings that would-be predators instinctively recognize and respect. Other markings are extraordinary, fool-the-eye camouflages, rendering the frog or toad nearly invisible in its own habitat or giving it an unappetizing appearance. In the gallery shown here (top row, from left) are the beautiful tree frog of Central America, with fiery eyes and toes that look as though they have enameled nails; the blue-legged strawberry frog of Costa Rica and Panama; and the crawfish frog, an Oklahoma native with a croak that sounds like a loud snore. Center row: the Indian red-backed frog; the dour-looking Surinam tree frog, with emerald-green markings that give it the appearance of a leaf; and the black-and-gold striped kassina of central Africa, with a voice sounding like a cork popping from a bottle. Bottom row: the golden mantella of Madagascar; the barking tree frog of the southeastern United States; and the painted reed frog of South Africa.

Tableau of Toads

The homely common toad at left has a prodigious appetite for insects and is much esteemed as a pest control. The giant toad of South America is recognized as such a killer of sugar beetles that it has been exported in great numbers to every cane-producing country in the world and has been credited with saving a large part of the world's annual sugar harvest. Its introduction into these areas has also been condemned, since it disrupts the local amphibian population, killing useful frogs. A killer of another sort is the Oriental fire-bellied toad (opposite), a native of eastern China and Korea. When threatened, it lies on its back, exposing its flame-colored underbelly, and exudes a foaming poison that may kill potential predators and will irritate the mucous membranes of humans who touch it and make the eyes water even without contact.

The bumpy-skinned common toad (above) will not cause warts in people who handle it, despite the claims of the old superstition. Not all members of the toad family are warty; they are, in fact, extremely varied in appearance, as the horned Cameroon toad of Africa attests (right). Its yellow dorsal skin is a leaflike disguise to convince predators that there is no toad underneath.

The Celebrated Jumping Frog of Calaveras County

by Mark Twain

As a young newspaper reporter in Virginia City, Nevada, in 1861, Samuel Clemens sold his first piece of fiction to a New York newspaper and signed it with a pen name, Mark Twain. The short story was "The Celebrated Jumping Frog of Calaveras County," and it brought its author and his byline immediate fame. In this, as in Tom Sawyer, Huckleberry Finn *and other works that confirmed him as America's leading humorist, Twain let his characters speak for themselves, retelling their favorite anecdotes in their own way. The narrator here takes his role seriously. He regards Jim Smiley, a compulsive gambler, and his famous frog as heroes of the highest order and the jumping contest as well worth putting on record.*

Well, thish-yer Smiley had rat-tarriers, and chicken cocks, and tom-cats and all them kind of things, till you couldn't rest, and you couldn't fetch nothing for him to bet on but he'd match you. He ketched a frog one day, and took him home, and said he calk'lated to edercate him; and so he never done nothing for three months but set in his back yard and learn that frog to jump. And you bet you he *did* learn him, too. He'd give him a little punch behind, and the next minute you'd see that frog whirling in the air like a doughnut—see him turn one summerset, or maybe a couple, if he got a good start, and come down flat-footed and all right, like a cat. He got him up so in the matter of ketching flies, and kept him in practice so constant, that he'd nail a fly every time as far as he could see him. Smiley said all a frog wanted was education, and he could do 'most anything—and I believe him. Why, I've seen him set Dan'l Webster down here on this floor—Dan'l Webster was the name of the frog—and sing out, "Flies, Dan'l, flies!" and quicker'n you could wink he'd spring straight up and snake a fly off'n the counter there, and flop down on the floor ag'in as solid as a gob of mud, and fall to scratching the side of his head with his hind foot as indifferent as if he hadn't no idea he'd been doin' any more'n any frog might do. You never see a frog so modest and straightfor'ard as he was, for all he was so gifted. And when it come to fair and square jumping on a dead level, he could get over more ground at one straddle than any animal of his breed you ever see. Jumping on a dead level was his strong suit, you understand; and when it come to that, Smiley would ante up money on him as long as he had a red. Smiley was monstrous proud of his frog, and well he might be, for fellers that had traveled and been everywheres, all said he laid over any frog that ever *they* see.

Well, Smiley kept the beast in a little lattice box, and he used to fetch him down town sometimes and lay for a bet. One day a feller—a stranger in the camp, he was—come across him with his box, and says:

"What might it be that you've got in the box?"

And Smiley says, sorter indifferent-like, "It might be a parrot, or it might be a canary, maybe, but it ain't—it's only just a frog."

And the feller took it, and looked at it careful, and turned it round this way and that, and says, "H'm—so 'tis. Well, what's *he* good for?"

"Well," Smiley says, easy and careless, "he's good enough for *one* thing, I should judge—he can outjump any frog in Calaveras County."

The feller took the box again, and took another long, particular look, and give it back to Smiley, and says, very deliberate, "Well," he says, "I don't see no p'ints about that frog that's any better'n any other frog."

"Maybe you don't," Smiley says. "Maybe you understand frogs and maybe you don't understand 'em; maybe you've had experience, and maybe you ain't only a amature, as it were. Anyways, I've got *my* opinion and I'll risk forty dollars that he can outjump any frog in Calaveras County."

And the feller studied a minute, and then says, kinder sad like, "Well, I'm only a stranger here, and I ain't got no frog; but if I had a frog, I'd bet you."

And then Smiley says, "That's all right—that's all right—if you'll hold my box a minute, I'll go and get you a frog." And so the feller took the box, and put up his forty dollars along with Smiley's and set down to wait.

So he set there a good while thinking and thinking to

North American bullfrog

hisself, and then he got the frog out and prized his mouth open and took a teaspoon and filled him full of quail shot—filled him pretty near up to his chin—and set him on the floor. Smiley he went to the swamp and slopped around in the mud for a long time, and finally he ketched a frog, and fetched him in, and give him to this feller, and says:

"Now, if you're ready, set him alongside of Dan'l, with his fore-paws just even with Dan'l's, and I'll give the word." Then he says, "One—two—three—jump!" and him and the feller touched up the frogs from behind, and the new frog hopped off, but Dan'l give a heave, and hysted up his shoulders—so—like a Frenchman, but it wa'n't no use—he couldn't budge; he was planted as solid as an anvil, and he couldn't no more stir than if he was anchored out. Smiley was a good deal surprised, and he was disgusted too, but he didn't have no idea what the matter was, of course.

The feller took the money and started away; and when he was going out at the door, he sorter jerked his thumb over his shoulders—this way—at Dan'l, and says again, very deliberate, "Well, *I* don't see no p'ints about that frog that's any better'n any other frog."

Smiley he stood scratching his head and looking down at Dan'l a long time, and at last he says, "I do wonder what in the nation that frog throw'd off for—I wonder if there ain't something the matter with him—he 'pears to look mighty baggy, somehow." And he ketched Dan'l by the nap of the neck, and lifted him up, and says, "Why, blame my cats, if he don't weigh five pound!" and turned him upside down and he belched out a double handful of shot. And then he see how it was, and he was the maddest man—he set the frog down and took out after that feller, but he never ketched him. . . .

124

Credits

Cover photograph—J. H. Robinson from Photo Researchers, Inc. 1—Tom McHugh from Photo Researchers, Inc. 5—Paul Chesley. 6—(left) R. E. Pelham from Bruce Coleman, Inc., (right) Alan Blank from Bruce Coleman, Inc. 7—J. H. Carmichael, Jr., from Bruce Coleman, Inc. 15—Nina Leen. 16—Nina Leen. 17—(top, left and right) Nina Leen, (bottom) Tom McHugh from Photo Researchers, Inc. 18—(left) Leonard Lee Rue III from Bruce Coleman, Inc., 18–19—Nina Leen. 20–21—Nina Leen. 22—C. Blank, National Audubon Society Collection, Photo Researchers, Inc. 23—(top and bottom) Nina Leen. 28–29—Nina Leen. 30—(top and bottom) Nina Leen. 31—(top) J. B. Blossom from Photo Researchers, Inc., (bottom) C. Blank from National Audubon Society Collection, Photo Researchers, Inc. 32—(left) Alan Blank from Bruce Coleman, Inc. 32–33—C. Blank, National Audubon Society Collection, Photo Researchers, Inc. 34—Tom McHugh from Photo Researchers, Inc. 35—(top and bottom) Nina Leen. 36–37—Dr. Robert S. Simmons. 38—(top) James Simon from Bruce Coleman, Inc., (bottom) Dr. Robert S. Simmons. 39—(top) J. McDonald from Bruce Coleman, Inc., (bottom) Jen & Des Bartlett from Bruce Coleman, Inc. 40—(top) Nina Leen, (bottom) H. Uible from Photo Researchers, Inc. 41—J. H. Robinson from Photo Researchers, Inc. 43—Dr. Robert S. Simmons. 44—Nina Leen. 45—(top) Tom McHugh for Baiyer River Sanctuary, Photo Researchers, Inc., (bottom) K. H. Switak from Photo Researchers, Inc. 46—J. B. Blossom from Photo Researchers, Inc. 47—Dr. Robert S. Simmons. 49—Tom Myers from Photo Researchers, Inc. 50—J. H. Carmichael, Jr., from Bruce Coleman, Inc. 51—(top) D. Lyons from Bruce Coleman, Inc., (bottom) Tom McHugh from Photo Researchers, Inc. 52—(top) A. Blank from National Audubon Society Collection, Photo Researchers, Inc., (bottom) Barbour, from Photo Researchers, Inc. 53—(top) Z. Leszczynski from *Animals Animals*, (bottom) Nina Leen. 56—Nina Leen. 57—(top) Norman Myers from Bruce Coleman, Inc., (bottom) Alan Blank from Bruce Coleman, Inc. 58—(top) Tom McHugh from Photo Researchers, Inc., (bottom) K. H. Switak from Photo Researchers, Inc. 59—J. B. Blossom from Photo Researchers, Inc. 60—D. Lyons from Bruce Coleman, Inc. 61—Jen & Des Bartlett from Bruce Coleman, Inc. 66—Nina Leen. 67—(left) G. D. Plage from Bruce Coleman, Inc., (right) Z. Leszczynski from *Animals Animals*. 68—(left) Tom McHugh for Steinhart Aquarium from Photo Researchers Inc., (right, top) A. Blank from Bruce Coleman, Inc., (right, center) E. R. Degginger from Bruce Coleman, Inc., (right, bottom) A. Blank from Bruce Coleman, Inc. 69—R. Brooks from Photo Researchers, Inc. 71—Nina Leen. 72–75—D. Hughes from Bruce Coleman, Inc. 76—A. E. Staffan from Photo Researchers, Inc. 77—Tom McHugh from Photo Researchers, Inc. 78—(left) L. M. Stone from Bruce Coleman, Inc., (top, right) M. Reeves from Photo Researchers, Inc., (bottom, right) M. P. Gadomski from Bruce Coleman, Inc. 79—(top, left) Leonard Lee Rue III from Bruce Coleman, Inc., (bottom, left) D. Overcash from Bruce Coleman, Inc., (top, right) D. Overcash from Bruce Coleman, Inc., (bottom, right) R. E. Pelham from Bruce Coleman, Inc. 83—Russ Kinne from Photo Researchers, Inc. 84–85—George Holton from Photo Researchers, Inc. 85—Andrew Rakoczy from National Audubon Society Collection, Photo Researchers, Inc. 86—A. Moldvay from Photo Researchers, Inc. 87—(top) J. Markham from Bruce Coleman, Inc., (bottom) A. Blank from Bruce Coleman, Inc. 88–89—C. Blank from National Audubon Society Collection, Photo Researchers, Inc. 89—(top and bottom) L. Dean, Time Inc. 90—C. Blank from Photo Researchers, Inc. 91—(left) George Holton from Photo Researchers, Inc., (right) J. H. Carmichael, Jr., from Bruce Coleman, Inc. 92—(left) R. L. Dunne from Bruce Coleman, Inc., (right) Russ Kinne from Photo Researchers, Inc. 93—(top and bottom) R. Morse, Time Inc. 94—(top) A. Blank from Bruce Coleman, Inc., (bottom) K. H. Switak from Photo Researchers, Inc. 95—J. Wallis from Bruce Coleman, Inc. 96—Bill Belknap, Rapho Div., Photo Researchers, Inc. 96–97—J. Simon from Photo Researchers, Inc. 99—M. F. Sopher from Bruce Coleman, Inc. 101—P. Caulfield from *Animals Animals*. 102—(top) R. Hermes, National Audubon Society Collection, Photo Researchers, Inc., (bottom) Wolfgang Bayer. 103—Wolfgang Bayer. 104–105—S. Wayman, Time Inc. 104—(bottom) Tom McHugh for Steinhart Aquarium, Photo Researchers, Inc. 105—(bottom) E. Hanumantha Rao from Photo Researchers, Inc. 107—Dr. Carl Gans. 109—Jane Burton from Bruce Coleman, Inc. 110—(top) Dr. Robert S. Simmons, (bottom) J. M. Burnley from Bruce Coleman, Inc. 111—(top) Dr. Robert S. Simmons, (bottom) A. Blank from Bruce Coleman, Inc. 113—Tom McHugh for the Dallas Zoo from Photo Researchers, Inc. 114—(top) Jane Burton from Bruce Coleman, Inc., (bottom) E. R. Degginger from Bruce Coleman, Inc. 115—(top) G. Shapira from Photo Researchers, Inc., (bottom) K. Brate from Photo Researchers, Inc. 116–117—Jane Burton from Bruce Coleman, Inc. 118—(left, top) Tom McHugh for the Atlanta Zoo, Photo Researchers, Inc., (left, center) Tom McHugh from Photo Researchers, Inc., (left, bottom) A. Blank from Bruce Coleman, Inc. 118—(right, top) Tom McHugh from Photo Researchers, Inc., (right, center) Russ Kinne from Photo Researchers, Inc., (right, bottom) Dr. Robert S. Simmons. 119—(top) Dr. Robert S. Simmons, (center) Jen & Des Bartlett from Bruce Coleman, Inc., (bottom) K. H. Switak from Photo Researchers, Inc. 120—(top) D. Guravich from Photo Researchers, Inc., (bottom) Tom McHugh for the Atlanta Zoo from Photo Researchers, Inc. 121—S. Bisserot from Bruce Coleman, Inc. 122—Louis Quitt from Photo Researchers, Inc. 128—Tom McHugh from Photo Researchers, Inc.

Photographs on endpapers are used courtesy of Time-Life Picture Agency and Russ Kinne and Stephen Dalton of Photo Researchers, Inc.

Film sequences on pages 8, 13, 19, 47, 61, 66 and 103 are from "Snakes of India," "Deadly American Snakes," "Green Ceilings of Borneo," "Deadly African Snakes" and "Crocodiles," programs in the Time-Life Television series *Wild, Wild World of Animals*.

MAP on page 98 is by Breck Trautwein.

ILLUSTRATION on page 9 courtesy of the Metropolitan Museum of Art, Anonymous Gift, 1944. The illustration on pages 10–11 is by Peter Zallinger, the illustration on page 12 is by Sy Barlowe, those on pages 25 and 27 are by Arnold Roth, the illustration on page 34 is by Chester S. Tarka, the illustration on pages 54–55 is by André Durenceau, the illustrations on pages 63, 64–65 and 125 are by John Groth. The woodcut on page 81 is by Claire Oldham, courtesy of The Cresset Press, London.

Bibliography

NOTE: Asterisk at the left means that a paperback volume is also listed in *Books in Print*.

Aymar, Brandt, *Treasury of Snake Lore*. Greenberg, 1956.

Barbour, R. W., *Reptiles and Amphibians: Their Habits and Adaptations*. Houghton Mifflin, 1929.

Barker, Will, *Familiar Reptiles and Amphibians of America*. Harper & Row, 1964.

Bellairs, Angus, *The Life of Reptiles*. Universe Books, 1970.

Caras, Roger, *Dangerous to Man*. Chilton Books, 1964.

Carr, Archie, *Handbook of Turtles*. Comstock, 1952.

————, and the editors of Time-Life Books, *The Reptiles*. Time-Life Books, 1963.

Cochran, Doris, *Living Amphibians of the World*. Doubleday, 1961.

Ditmars, Raymond L., *Reptiles of the World*. The Macmillan Company, 1946.

————, *Snakes of the World*. The Macmillan Company, 1966.

Goin, C., and Goin, O., *Introduction to Herpetology*. W. H. Freeman, 1971.

Grzimek, Bernhard, *Grzimek's Animal Life Encyclopedia*. Vols. V and VI. Van Nostrand Reinhold, 1974, 1975.

Isemonger, R. M., *Snakes of Africa*. Thomas Nelson, 1962.

*Krutch, Joseph, *Voice of the Desert*. William Morrow, 1955.

Mertens, Robert, *The World of Amphibians*. McGraw-Hill, 1960.

Minton, Sherman A., Jr., and Minton, Madge Rutherford, *Giant Reptiles*. Charles Scribner's Sons, 1973.

*————, *Venomous Reptiles*. Charles Scribner's Sons, 1969.

Morris, Ramona, and Morris, Desmond, *Men and Snakes*. McGraw-Hill, 1965.

Neill, Wilfred, *The Last of the Ruling Reptiles*. Columbia University Press, 1971.

Noël-Hume, Ivor, and Noël-Hume, Audrey, *Tortoises, Terrapins and Turtles*. Frederick Muller, 1954.

*Oliver, James A., *Snakes in Fact and Fiction*. The Macmillan Company, 1959.

Parker, H. W., *Snakes*. W. W. Norton, 1963.

Pope, Clifford H., *The Giant Snakes*. Alfred A. Knopf, 1961.

————, *The Reptile World*. Alfred A. Knopf, 1955.

————, *Snakes Alive*. The Viking Press, 1942.

Richardson, Maurice, *The Fascination of Reptiles*. Hill & Wang, 1972.

Schmidt, Karl P., and Inger, Robert F., *Living Reptiles of the World*. Doubleday, 1957.

Smyth, H., *Amphibians and Their Ways*. The Macmillan Company, 1962.

*Zim, Herbert S., and Smith, Hobart M., *Reptiles and Amphibians*. Golden Press, 1953.

Index

128

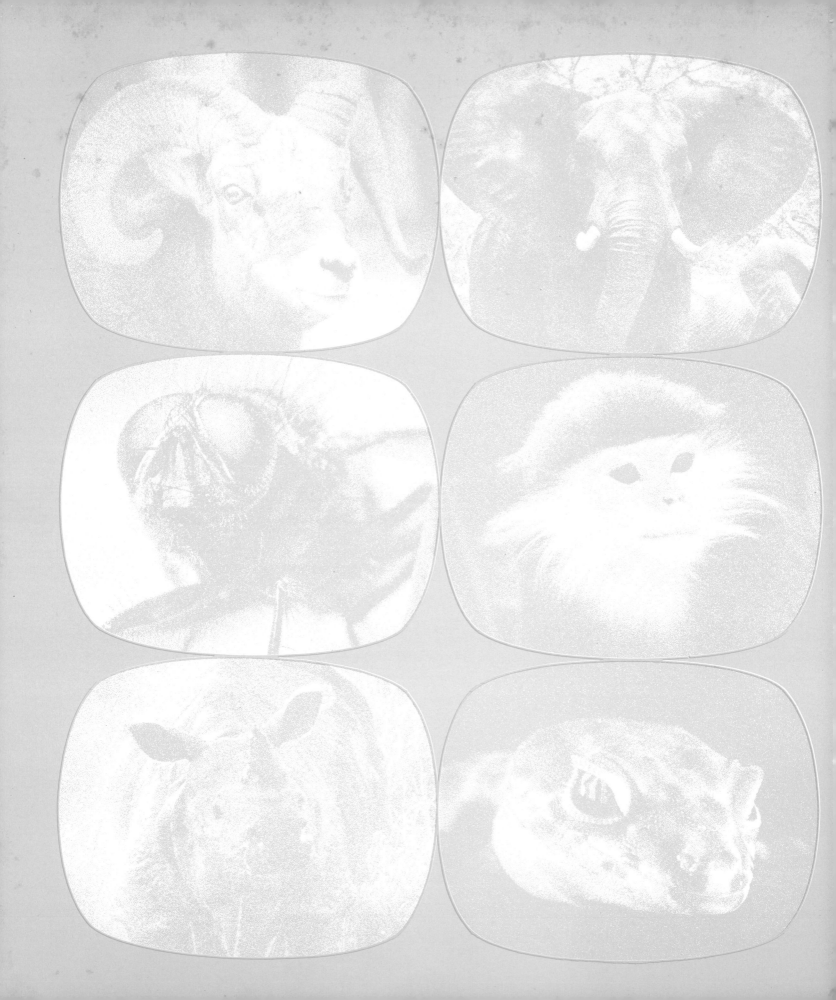